D0358752

NEW PARISH PRAYERS

By the same author

PARISH PRAYERS (Editor)

CONTEMPORARY PARISH PRAYERS (Editor)

NEW EVERY MORNING (Editor)
(BBC Publications)

PREACHING AT THE PARISH COMMUNION
(Mowbrays)

PREACHING THROUGH THE CHRISTIAN YEAR
(Mowbrays)

HYMNS THAT LIVE

PRAYERS THAT LIVE
(SPCK)

NEW PARISH PRAYERS

Compiled and edited
by
FRANK COLQUHOUN

With a Foreword by
THE RIGHT REVEREND LORD COGGAN

HODDER AND STOUGHTON
LONDON SYDNEY AUCKLAND TORONTO

British Library Cataloguing in Publication Data

New parish prayers.
1. Church of England – Prayer-books and devotions
I. Colquhoun, Frank
264'.03 BX5145

ISBN 0-340-27237-6

Printed in Great Britain for Hodder and Stoughton Limited, Mill Road, Dunton Green, Sevenoaks, Kent by St Edmundsbury Press, Bury St Edmunds, Suffolk. Photoset by Rowland Phototypesetting Limited, Bury St Edmunds, Suffolk. Hodder and Stoughton Editorial Office: 47 Bedford Square, London WC1B 3DP.

CONTENTS

FOREWORD
BY THE RIGHT REVEREND LORD COGGAN

I AM glad that there is now a third volume of prayers to put alongside the former two, *Parish Prayers* and *Contemporary Parish Prayers*, which Canon Colquhoun has given us and which I have noticed in so many churches in this country and abroad. We owe Canon Colquhoun a deep debt of gratitude for his work in this field over many years.

This third book relies, as did the other two, on a wide variety of sources. Among others, it contains many of the editor's own prayers and gathers riches from our sister Church in the United States – it is good that we should share our treasure within our own communion and beyond it.

I hope that the book will be used by many in their private devotions. I hope even more earnestly that it will be used by those, clerical and lay, who have the responsibility of leading public worship. Few are adept at praying in public *ex tempore* in a manner worthy of public worship. May this book save us from the shoddy and the second-rate, and be used by the Holy Spirit to deepen the prayer life of the Church.

Donald Coggan

AUTHOR'S PREFACE

THIS collection of prayers is a sequel to my *Contemporary Parish Prayers*, published in 1975. It consists in part of material which I have gathered together since that time from a variety of sources, and in part of a considerable number of new prayers written for this collection, including just over a hundred prayers of my own. All the prayers are in modern idiom and so are suitable for use with the Alternative Service Book.

In general the prayers cover a broader field than those in the previous publication. For this reason I hope the book may serve a wider purpose and prove useful not only in church work in the narrower sense but also in schools, colleges, youth clubs, and the like. Some of the material is also suitable for personal devotion.

I am deeply grateful to Bishop Donald Coggan for contributing the foreword to this volume, as he did to its predecessor and to *Parish Prayers* (1967). The interest he has shown in these undertakings has been a great encouragement to me in my work. Above all, I value the friendship he has shared with me over a long period of years.

I must also express my thanks to those who have written prayers for this book and without whose contributions it would never have been completed: Canon Michael Botting, Canon Maurice Burrell, the Rev. Llewellyn Cumings, Bishop Timothy Dudley-Smith, the Rev. Christopher Idle, Canon Basil Naylor, the Rev. Martin Parsons, Canon John Poulton, the Rev. Stanley Pritchard (of the Church of Scotland) and Provost Alan Warren. In addition, I am grateful to Canon John Kingsnorth of the United Society for the Propagation of the Gospel for allowing me to reproduce prayers written by him for the society's publications, and to the Rev. Raymond Maynard for giving me access to prayers in his own personal collection.

I have taken advantage of the opportunity afforded me of including many prayers from the newly revised Book of Common Prayer (1977) of the Episcopal Church of the United States of America. This book contains a larger selection of prayers and intercessions than our own ASB and embodies some very useful material.

The authorship of a good many of the prayers included in the following pages is unknown to me, and such prayers bear no ascription. An asterisk (*) has been added to the ascription of those prayers which have been altered or shortened. Prayers described as *Adapted* have been derived from various sources, known and unknown, and have been either considerably modified or more or less rewritten by myself. If in any instance I have ascribed prayers to wrong sources, or infringed any copyrights, I offer my apology to those concerned and will make amends in any subsequent edition. A list of Acknowledgments will be found at the end of the volume.

FRANK COLQUHOUN

Bexhill-on-Sea,
January 1982

I
BEFORE AND AFTER PRAYER

INTRODUCTION TO WORSHIP

True worship **1**

FATHER, help us to worship you in spirit and in truth;
that our consciences may be quickened by your holiness,
our minds nourished by your truth,
our imaginations purified by your beauty,
our hearts opened to your love,
our wills surrendered to your purpose;
and may all this be gathered up in adoration
as we ascribe glory, praise and honour to you alone,
through Jesus Christ our Lord.

Adapted from William Temple

2

Holy, righteous, and merciful God, enable us by your grace to offer you true worship and joyful service.

Cleanse our minds and free our consciences from the things that hide you from us, and unite us one with another in the fellowship of the Spirit; through Christ, our Lord and our Redeemer.

The approach to worship **3**

Heavenly Father, we come together as members of your family
to offer you our praise and thanksgiving,
to hear and receive your holy Word,
to bring before you the needs of the world,

to seek your mercy and forgiveness,
and to offer our lives anew to your service.
Graciously accept us in your Son Jesus Christ
and pour upon us your abundant blessing,
to the glory of your great name. *Adapted*

4

Almighty God, in whom we live and move and have our being, who made us for yourself, so that our hearts are restless till they rest in you:

we give you thanks for every mercy granted to us in times past, and for your presence with us at this hour.

As here we seek to rededicate our life and work to you, grant us purity of heart and strength of purpose, that no selfish passion may hinder us from knowing your will, no weakness from doing it; but that in your light we may see light clearly, and in your service find our perfect freedom; through Jesus Christ our Lord. *After St Augustine*

5

Give us, our Father, a sense of your presence
as we gather now for worship.
Grant us gratitude as we remember your goodness,
penitence as we remember our sins,
and joy as we remember your love;
and enable us to lift up our hearts
in humble prayer and fervent praise;
through Jesus Christ our Lord.

6

Give us grace, O God, in this act of worship
to serve you with gladness,
to sing to you a new song,

to give much and to receive much;
and draw us into closer fellowship with you
and with one another,
through your Son our Saviour Jesus Christ.

Christopher Idle

7

Help us, O Lord, to use the time before each service in preparation of heart and mind; that no wrong attitudes or dullness of spirit may make our worship unworthy, our fellowship unreal, or rob you of the glory that is your due; through Jesus Christ our Lord. *Christopher Idle*

Silence and song **8**

Father, we come to you now in silence, yet shouting for joy.

We come in silence overawed by the thought of your love for us; for you loved us so much that you gave your only Son to suffer and die for us.

Yet to think that you love us like that makes us long to break our silence: to shout for joy and sing your praise.

You have given us new birth into a living hope through the resurrection of Jesus Christ from the dead. In him we are ransomed, healed, restored, forgiven.

Father, accept our worship and praise, both silent and spoken, to the glory of your holy name. *Adapted*

A holy priesthood **9**

Eternal God, you have called your Church
to be a holy priesthood,
that it may offer to you spiritual sacrifices,
acceptable through Jesus Christ.
Receive our prayers and praises,

the devotion of our hearts
and the dedication of our lives;
and may our worship redound to your great glory,
now and always. *Frank Colquhoun*

The house of the Lord **10**

Father, may we be glad when it is said to us,
"Let us go to the house of the Lord!"
Let it be our delight as well as our duty
to worship you in the fellowship of the Church.
Prepare us in mind and spirit for our worship,
and tune our hearts to sing your praise.
May we receive all that you have to give to us,
and offer all that you require from us;
and may our lives as well as our lips glorify you,
through Christ our Lord. *Frank Colquhoun*

11

All your works magnify you, O Lord,
and your faithful servants extol your name.
With grateful hearts we share in their praises
and bow in reverence before your throne.
Receive and sanctify the worship
we offer now in this house of prayer,
and make it an acceptable sacrifice
to your honour and glory;
through Jesus Christ our Lord. *Frank Colquhoun*

BEFORE PRAYER

The spirit of prayer **12**

GIVE us grace, Almighty Father, to address you with all our hearts as well as with our lips.

You are everywhere present: from you no secrets can be hidden.

Teach us to fix our thoughts on you, reverently and with love, so that our prayers are not in vain, but are acceptable to you, now and always; through Jesus Christ our Lord.

Adapted from Jane Austen

13

O Lord, hear our prayers,
not according to the poverty of our asking
but according to the richness of your grace,
so that our lives may conform to those desires
which accord with your will;
through Jesus Christ our Lord. *Reinhold Niebuhr*

14

Let not our souls be busy inns, O Christ, that have no room for you, but quiet houses of prayer and praise where you may find fit company; where the needful cares of life are wisely ordered and put away, and where holy thoughts pass up and down, and fervent longings watch and await your coming, our beloved Saviour and our Lord.

15

O Lord our God, great, eternal, wonderful,
utterly to be trusted,
you welcome all who come to you.
Forgive our sins, secret and open,
and cleanse us of every thought
which is foreign to your love;
that our hearts and minds may be at peace,
and we may bring our prayers to you
confidently and without fear;
through Jesus Christ our Lord. *Guild of Health*

The presence of God **16**

Father, as we turn aside from the busy world
with its clamour and distractions,
quieten our hearts in your presence,
that we may be still and know that you are God,
our God, now and for ever,
through Jesus Christ our Lord. *Frank Colquhoun*

17

We thank you, Lord Christ, for the promise of your presence to the two or three who gather in your name.

Help us to remember that you are with us now as we meet to pray.

Make us of one heart and mind, that we may agree in what we ask; and as we offer our petitions in your name, so may we pray in accordance with your will, and glorify our Father in heaven. *Based on Matthew 18. 19, 20*

18

Lord, help us to understand that
because of your coming to us
in the power of the Holy Spirit,
prayer is no longer the knocking at a door
but the opening of a window. *Alan Warren*

19

Let us remember that God is with us now.
There is no place where God is not.
Wherever we go, there God is.
Now and always he encompasses us,
looks upon us with his mercy,
and is ready to hear us when we call.
Therefore let us pray. *Adapted*

Intercession **20**

Risen and ascended Lord, you live for ever to intercede for us.

Graciously assist us as we now join in intercession for others.

Deepen our understanding of your great love for them and for us; deliver us from self-concern; and make us channels of your grace to those for whom we pray, to the glory of your name. *Adapted*

CONCLUDING PRAYERS

After divine service **21**

HEAVENLY Father, you have promised to hear us when we ask in the name of your Son: accept and fulfil our petitions, we pray, not as we ask in our ignorance, nor as we deserve in our sinfulness, but as you know and love us in your Son Jesus Christ our Lord.

Episcopal Church, U.S.A.

22

O Lord our God, accept the prayers of your people; and in the multitude of your mercies look with compassion upon us and all who turn to you for help; for you are gracious, O lover of souls, and to you we give glory, Father, Son, and Holy Spirit, now and for ever.

Episcopal Church, U.S.A.

23

Father, as we go forth from this service in church,
strengthen us for service in the world;
that the words we have heard and said and sung
may find expression in our daily life and work,
to the glory of your holy name. *Frank Colquhoun*

Committal **24**

To your care and protection, O Lord,
we now commit ourselves.
Of your goodness forgive us;
with your love inspire us;
by your Spirit guide us;
and in your mercy keep us,
now and always.

25

Eternal God and Father, help us to entrust
the past to your mercy,
the present to your love,
and the future to your wisdom,
in the name of Jesus Christ our Lord,
who is the same yesterday, and today,
and for ever.

Short closing prayers **26**

O God, grant that always,
at all times and in all places,
in things both great and small,
we may do your good and perfect will,
and continue your faithful servants
to the end of our lives;
through Jesus Christ our Lord.

27

Grant, O Lord, that your love
may so fill our lives that we may count
nothing too small to do for you,
nothing too much to give,
and nothing too hard to bear,
for Jesus Christ's sake. *St. Ignatius Loyola*

28

Lord, may we live in faith,
walk in love,
and be renewed in hope,
until the world reflects your glory
and you are all in all.

29

Lord, of your great mercy
teach us what we know not,
grant us what we have not,
make us what we are not,
and all for your glory.

Doxologies 30

Glory be to God our Father,
creator, sustainer, Lord of all things.
Glory be to Jesus Christ our Saviour,
born in humility, crucified in weakness,
risen in power, reigning in majesty.
Glory be to the Holy Spirit the Comforter,
sanctifying, cleansing, strengthening,
uniting us in the family of the Church.
Glory be to the Father, Son, and Holy Spirit,
one God for ever and ever.

31

Yours is the majesty, O Lord our God,
Father, Son, and Holy Spirit;
yours is the kingdom and the power;
yours be the glory now and for evermore.

32

Eternal God, above all your manifold gifts of grace we worship and adore you for yourself:

for your holiness and justice,
for your majesty and power,
for your love and mercy.

Glory be to you, O God, for all that you are,
Father, Son, and Holy Spirit,
one God, and our God, for ever and ever.

33

Glory be to you, O God our Creator.
Glory be to you, O Jesus our Redeemer.
Glory be to you, O Holy Spirit, our Sanctifier.
Glory be to the Father, the Son, and the Holy Spirit,
both now and for evermore.

After Thomas Wilson

Benedictions **34**

The blessing of the Lord rest and remain upon all his people, in every land, of every tongue;

the Lord meet in mercy all who seek him;
the Lord comfort all who suffer and mourn;
the Lord hasten his coming, and give us his people peace by all means, now and for ever. *Handley C. G. Moule*

35

May God sustain you in all your works
and in all your ways;
make you humble, just, and true;
strengthen you in holiness and righteousness;
and fill your home with love and peace.
And may the blessing of God Almighty,
the Father, the Son, and the Holy Spirit,
rest upon you and remain with you always.

36

God be with you in your going out and in your coming in.
God be with you in your work and in your leisure.
God be with you in life's hills and in its valleys.
God be with you in company and in solitude.
God be with you in all your pilgrimage and at its end.
And the blessing of God the Father, Son, and Holy Spirit abide with you always.

Stanley Pritchard

37

May the love of God enfold you;
may the mercy of God absolve you;
may the strength of God support you;
may the peace of God console you;
and may the blessing of God Almighty,
Father, Son, and Holy Spirit,
be with you now and evermore.

Frank Colquhoun

II
THANKSGIVINGS

GENERAL

General thanksgivings **38**

ACCEPT, O Lord, our praise and thanks for all that you have done for us.

We thank you for the splendour of the whole creation, for the beauty of this world, for the wonder of life, and for the mystery of love.

We thank you for the blessing of family and friends, and for the loving care which surrounds us on every side.

We thank you for setting us tasks which demand our best efforts, and for leading us to accomplishments which satisfy and delight us.

We thank you also for those disappointments and failures that lead us to acknowledge our dependence on you alone.

Above all, we thank you for your Son Jesus Christ; for the truth of his Word and the example of his life; for his steadfast obedience, by which he overcame temptation; for his dying, through which he overcame death; and for his rising to life again, in which we are raised to the life of your kingdom.

Grant us the gift of your Spirit, that we may know him and make him known; and through him, at all times and in all places, may give thanks to you in all things.

Episcopal Church, U.S.A.

39

Almighty God, Father of all mercies and fountain of all goodness, we praise you for all your gifts to us and to all men.

We thank you for our life and for the blessings of health and strength.

We thank you for all the affections and love we meet in our daily life, for the tasks and responsibilities which relate us to those around us.

Help us to extend our concern to those far off, and make us mindful that we have been given means of doing good.

We give thanks for every measure by which you have taught us your truth and have brought our life into conformity to your will.

We ask that no ignorance or sin may turn our blessings into curses.

Give us such a lively sense of your goodness that we may devote ourselves to your will and service; so that loving you, we may find the way to an increasing love and brotherly communion with all your children. *Reinhold Niebuhr*

40

We thank you, O Lord, for all those good things which are in our world and in our lives through your great love and mercy.

Save us from being ungrateful.

Save us from magnifying our troubles and forgetting our blessings.

Give us strength of spirit to rise into joyfulness of heart; and by your help may we learn to live as those who have trusted in the promises of good which are incarnate in Jesus, and who know that in the end love must conquer all.

*A. Herbert Gray**

41

Eternal God, maker of all things, we praise and thank you for all the blessings and joys of life:

for those we love, for friendship, for those who serve and help us and supply our needs;

for the gift of sight and hearing, and for health and strength;

for all who devote themselves to the service of their fellows in the ministry of healing;
for writers, artists and musicians whose work has brought beauty into our souls;
for all those men and women whose ideals have brought nobility and dignity into human life;
for all who have kept before their eyes the vision of the kingdom of God.

Above all, we thank you for your love in creating us; for the redemption and healing of all the ills of life through the Passion and resurrection of your Son; and for the gift of your Holy Spirit.

For these and all other joys in life, O God, we praise and bless you, we give you thanks, through Jesus Christ our Lord. *Guild of Health*

42

Our gracious God and Father, creator of all that is good, we thank you for the gift of life, for the wonder of the world in which you have placed us, and for all the blessings you so freely lavish upon us your children.

Forgive us that too often we take your gifts for granted and think so little of the Giver.

Help us to recognize your hand in the ordinary things of life, and never to be ungrateful for food and clothing, work and recreation, health and home, family and friends.

So may we live from day to day in the knowledge of your love and goodness, giving thanks always for all things, in the name of Jesus Christ our Lord. *Frank Colquhoun*

43

Heavenly Father, we come to you in the multitude of your mercies to offer you our thanks for all the gifts you have so richly bestowed upon us.

We thank you especially for health of mind and body,
for home and family and friends,
for literature, art and music,
for the bountiful world in which we live.

Help us to use your gifts wisely, faithfully and generously, that we may show our gratitude in deed and not in word only, and glorify you in our lives as well as with our lips; through Jesus Christ our Lord.

God's many gifts **44**

Almighty God, more generous than any father,
more loving than any family,
we stand amazed at the many gifts
you shower upon your people.
You give freely and willingly,
but always with regard for our ability to receive.
You give daily gifts,
teaching us to trust for tomorrow.
You give gifts to us through each other,
so that we learn to share.
You give through our own efforts,
respecting our independence.
How thoughtfully you offer all you give!
So continue, Lord.
We make our thanksgiving in Christ's name.

*Prayer for Christian Unity 1981**

45

Eternal God, the refuge and help of all your children,
we praise you for all you have given us,
for all you have done for us,
for all that you are to us.
In our weakness you are strength,
in our darkness you are light,

in our sorrow you are comfort and peace.
We cannot number your blessings,
  we cannot declare your love.
For all your goodness we bless you.
May we live as in your presence,
  and love the things that you love,
  and serve you in our daily lives;
through Jesus Christ our Lord.

Adapted from the prayer of St. Boniface

Divine Praises **46**

Blessed be God,
  who made men and women to share his love
  and the planet earth to be their home.
Blessed is Jesus,
  who emptied himself to become our brother,
  who died and who rose and who lives for ever.
Blessed the Spirit
  in his ever coming to the People of God,
  to fashion within them the life of their Lord.
Blessed is Mary,
  the mother of Jesus and of his people,
  model of all who are saved by his grace.
Blessed the Saints,
  the heroes of faith who fought and endured,
  who mirrored the myriad faces of God.
Blessed the Church,
  spanning all ages and embracing all nations,
  the city of hope in a world of despair.
Blessed my Brother,
  of differing speech and differing race,
  one with me in the household of faith.

Blessed the End,
  when the kingdom shall come
  and the Bride in her glory be joined to her Lord.

John Kingsnorth

The problem of giving thanks **47**

Lord, we love to be independent, and we find it hard to give thanks for everything that happens to us, everything that comes our way.

We want to feel that we have deserved success and a home and friends and honourable work; and so sometimes our thanksgivings ring false: just words that we take on our lips without meaning, without understanding.

We are not ungrateful, but we expect our due. We feel we have earned our place in society, and that by our own labours, our own thinking, our own vision, we have got where we are. We accept our gifts as our right.

So we forget that the whole earth is yours, and you gave it to us. We forget that the breath of life is your gift, and you made us living souls. We forget that our best purposes are yours, and that you have inspired us to achievement and strengthened us for fulfilment.

Give us therefore a grateful heart, O Lord, that we may offer our thanks with gladness and understanding, mindful that all things come from you, and that without you we have nothing and are nothing. *Stanley Pritchard*

Forgotten things **48**

Father of all mercies, we now call to mind with gratitude
  things for which we so often forget to give thanks.
We thank you for our ordinary everyday blessings as well as
    for life's special mercies;
  for our work as well as for our leisure;
  for the rain as well as for the sunshine.

We thank you for saving us from hidden and unknown perils;
for the sufferings and sorrows which have drawn us nearer to yourself;
for the lessons we have learned in life's dark valleys, its crises and sorrows and conflicts.
We thank you for your providential ordering of our steps;
for not granting us some of the things we prayed for;
for overruling our failures and mistakes for our good, and for your glory.
Of these things, our Father, keep us ever mindful,
and for these things accept our thanks;
through Jesus Christ our Lord. *Frank Colquhoun*

A LITANY OF THANKSGIVING

49

LET us give thanks to God our Father for all his gifts so freely bestowed upon us.

For the beauty and wonder of your creation, in earth and sky and sea,

We thank you, Lord.

For all that is gracious in the lives of men and women, revealing the image of Christ,

We thank you, Lord.

For our daily food and drink, our homes and families, and our friends,

We thank you, Lord.

For minds to think, and hearts to love, and hands to serve,

We thank you, Lord.

For health and strength to work, and leisure to rest and play,

We thank you, Lord.

For the brave and courageous, who are patient in suffering and faithful in adversity,

We thank you, Lord.

For all valiant seekers after truth, liberty, and justice,

We thank you, Lord.

For the communion of saints, in all times and places,

We thank you, Lord.

Above all, we give you thanks for the great mercies and promises given to us in Christ Jesus our Lord;

To him be praise and glory, with you, O Father, and the Holy Spirit, now and for ever. Amen.

Episcopal Church, U.S.A.

THANKSGIVINGS FOR PARTICULAR SUBJECTS

For the Church **50**

LORD God, our heavenly Father,
we give thanks for the Church of Jesus Christ,
the mother of saints and prophets
and millions of unsung lovely and loving souls,
reaching in our day to the ends of the earth
and proclaiming Jesus as Lord and Saviour of all the world.

We give thanks for those whose lives
are devoted to the service of others:
those who heal the sick and relieve mental suffering,
those who teach with devotion and skill,
those who care for the hungry, the homeless, and the refugee.

We give thanks for the Church's saints, known and unknown,
and for the dedicated lives of all faithful souls.
Grant us grace, O Lord, to follow in their footsteps,
that we may know the ultimate joy of meeting with them
in your eternal kingdom,
through your grace, and to your glory.

John Kingsnorth

For the mission of the Church **51**

Almighty God, you sent your Son Jesus Christ to reconcile the world to yourself: we praise and bless you for those whom you have sent in the power of the Spirit to preach the gospel to all nations.

We thank you that in all parts of the earth a community of love has been gathered together by their prayers and labours, and that in every place your servants call upon your name; for the kingdom and the power and the glory are yours for ever. *Episcopal Church, U.S.A.*

52

We thank you, Lord God, for the faith and courage of those men and women who, from the days of the apostles, have preached the gospel of the living Christ and have built up your Church in every land.

We thank you for those who stood firm in the face of persecution;

for those who brought the good news to these islands;

and for those who have gone forth from us as witnesses for our Lord in other lands.

Help us to realize that we are part of your great Church universal; keep us faithful to our trust; and make us the agents of your kingdom in the world of our day, for the glory of your name.

For the Bible **53**

O God, we thank you on this day for the sacred scriptures; for the comfort the Bible has brought to the sorrowful, for guidance offered to the bewildered, for its gracious promises to the uncertain, for its strength given to the weak, and for its progressive revelation of yourself.

We thank you for the men of God who speak to us still from its pages, and for the men of God whose learning has made those pages live.

We thank you most of all that it reveals to us your Son, the Word made flesh.

Help us to ponder this record of your ways with men, that

your Word may be indeed a lamp to our feet and a light to our path; through Jesus Christ our Lord.

Leslie D. Weatherhead

For spiritual mercies **54**

O Lord our God, we praise you, we bless you,
we give you thanks for your immeasurable goodness
  to those who believe in you.
We thank you for having loved us
  to the point of having sent your Son to redeem us.
In him we have seen your face,
  in him we have heard your Word.
Through him we have received your Spirit
  and become your children.
From him we have known your plan
  and learned to call you Father.
For your immeasurable goodness to us,
  for the love that draws us together and unites us,
we praise you, we bless you, we give you thanks,
  O Lord our God.

Adapted

For creation **55**

Almighty God, our Creator and Redeemer,
we praise you for all your wonderful works,
  for the beauty and bounty of the world around us,
  for everything you have given us so richly to enjoy.
We bless you for our own creation
as men and women made in your image,
  with minds to know you,
  hearts to love you,
  and wills to obey you.
Accept, O God, this our praise and thanksgiving,
and to your name be honour and glory for evermore.

Frank Colquhoun

For the beauty of the earth **56**

We give you thanks, most gracious God, for the beauty of earth and sky and sea; for the richness of mountains, plains and rivers; for the songs of birds and the loveliness of flowers.

We praise you for these good gifts, and pray that we may safeguard them for posterity.

Grant that we may continue to grow in our grateful enjoyment of your abundant creation, to the honour and glory of your name, now and for ever. *Episcopal Church, U.S.A.*

For books and the printed word **57**

Father, we thank you for the gift of language, and for the written word.

We thank you for writers, publishers and printers, for books and libraries, and for the spread of knowledge and the sharing of experience which come to us through the printed page.

We thank you for the books which have helped to shape our lives and to mould our tastes and values; that have furnished our minds, spoken to our hearts, enriched or entertained us, both in health and sickness.

Teach us to value literacy and to use it rightly; through him whose words are words of life, our Saviour Jesus Christ.

Timothy Dudley-Smith

For life's simple joys **58**

We thank you, our Father, for all the good gifts around us which add so much joy to our daily lives:

for the sun that warms us and the air that gives us life;
for the loveliness of the natural world;
for the changing seasons, each in its order beautiful;
for our homes and families and friends;
for health of body and soundness of mind;

for music and books and works of art;
for the land of our birth, the land we love;
for the lives and examples of good and saintly souls.

Father, for these manifold blessings and for all your love we give you heartfelt thanks, through Jesus Christ our Lord.

Adapted

For benefactors **59**

Father, we remember with gratitude those who use the gifts with which you have enriched their lives to benefit others:

those who promote and encourage art and music;
those through whose endowments knowledge is increased and made freely available;
those who enable charitable organizations to continue their works of mercy;
those who ensure that the churches maintain their witness and that the gospel is offered without price;
those who make it possible for men to explore the secrets of the universe and share with others the healing mysteries.

From those to whom much is given, much will be expected. May they be wise in the use of their gifts, offering them humbly without hope of gain, or self-seeking, or desire for recognition.

Stanley Pritchard

For a church centenary or anniversary **60**

Great is your faithfulness, O God our Father, and great is our joy at this time as we celebrate the *centenary* of this church, built for your glory and dedicated to . . .

We thank you for the witness it has maintained down the years as a centre of Christian worship and witness, teaching and service;

for all who have loyally served it as clergy and laity;

for the continuance of its life and work at the present time.

Accept our thanksgiving, O God; multiply your blessings upon us today; and lead us forward in the power of your Spirit to fresh ventures of faith in the days to come; through Jesus Christ our Lord. *Frank Colquhoun*

For a college or school foundation **61**

We give you thanks, Lord God, for those through whose vision, faith and generosity this *college* was founded, and for all who in later years have given their energies and resources to further the ideals of its founders.

We thank you for men and women of learning who as teachers or students have advanced the frontiers of knowledge, and given service to their fellow men in our nation and in other parts of the world;

for our sister colleges, and all places of education in this country and overseas, and for their fellowship in the same ideals of learning and service;

for the blessings of life itself, for the skills of mind and hand, and for the joy of search for truth.

Accept, O God, this our thanksgiving, through Jesus Christ our Lord. *Basil Naylor*

For the departed **62**

We give thanks to you, our Father,
for all your servants departed this life in your faith and fear;
for the memory of their words and deeds;
for the sure and certain hope of reunion with them hereafter;
for the joy that is now theirs, free from earth's sin and sorrow;
and for our communion with them in your Son,
Jesus Christ our Lord. *Adapted*

For the saints of our own nation **63**

As we bless you, O Lord, for all the saints who from their labours rest, we thank you for the saints of our own nation:

for those who in early days pioneered the gospel in our land;

for those who kept the lamp of faith burning in times of spiritual darkness;

for those who bravely suffered martyrdom for the truth they loved;

for those who went as messengers of Christ to distant lands to share the good news with others;

for those who fought the battle for social righteousness and cared for the poor and oppressed.

Keep us ever mindful, O God, of the example of these your saints, and make us more worthy to follow in their steps; through Jesus Christ our Lord. *Frank Colquhoun*

For those who serve the community **64**

We thank you, our Father, for those whose work sustains our nation, and this community in which we live; for all who create the wealth by which we trade, for those who grow and provide our food, or who in industry, commerce and transport bring it to our homes.

We thank you for those who, day and night, maintain the public services; for the police, for those who respond to emergencies, and for all whose work is in health or healing or social care.

Teach us to remember that all our lives depend upon the work of many minds and hands; and we pray that we may live thankfully and in unity as members of one human family; through Jesus Christ our Lord.

Timothy Dudley-Smith

For health and medical service **65**

We thank you, O Lord God, for the gift of health of body, mind and spirit; for the measure of harmony within us by which a thousand factors work together to produce freedom from pain and distress of mind.

We thank you for every ministry of healing offered to those who suffer:

for the hospitals of our land and those who staff them;

for the skill of doctors, surgeons and psychiatrists, for dental surgeons, nurses, physiotherapists, masseurs and technicians;

for the discovery of anaesthetics and anodynes, for curative drugs, for psychological methods, and for every means of making men whole.

Show us how to prevent the burden of suffering which weighs on so many lives, that the humanity for which Christ died may be indeed redeemed in body, mind and spirit. We ask it in his name. *Leslie D. Weatherhead*

For our mental health **66**

Lord of our life, we thank you for the health you have given us, and especially for health of mind:

for our powers of intellect, judgment, memory, and imagination;

for the capacity to think and reason, to study and learn;

and for the inner light of your Spirit illuminating our understanding.

For this, O God, accept our gratitude; and give us a deeper and increasing knowledge of yourself, that we may learn to love you with all our mind; through Jesus Christ our Lord.

Frank Colquhoun

For other thanksgivings, see index of subjects

III
THE CHURCH'S YEAR

ADVENT

The coming of Christ **67**

MERCIFUL God, who sent your messengers the prophets to preach repentance and prepare the way of our salvation: give us grace to heed their warnings and forsake our sins, that we may greet with joy the coming of Jesus Christ our Redeemer; who lives and reigns with you and the Holy Spirit, now and for ever. *Episcopal Church, U.S.A.*

68

Almighty God, your prophets of old
heralded the coming of the Christ,
and in the fullness of time he came,
according to your word,
born of a woman that he might take our flesh
and share our humanity.
All praise to you, our Father,
for the coming of Jesus your Son;
all glory and honour to your name,
now and for ever. *Frank Colquhoun*

69

O God, you sent your Son into the world
to be the Saviour of all who believe,
and promised that he will come again to be our judge:
increase in us the attitude of watchfulness and prayer,
so that we may always be ready to meet him,
with our lamps trimmed and burning
and our lives active in his service,
to the glory of your name. *Llewellyn Cumings*

70

Give us grace, O Lord, to live each day
as if it were the day of your coming.
May we be urgent to prepare your way
by fighting all evil,
by preaching the gospel,
by feeding the hungry,
by releasing the oppressed,
and by healing the sick.
So may we hasten the triumph of your kingdom,
and bring glory to your name. *John Kingsnorth*

The Bible **71**

We thank you, our Father, that the Christian way in which we walk is no uncharted path, but a road beaten hard by the footsteps of saints, apostles, prophets and martyrs.

We thank you for the signposts and danger signals with which the path is marked and which may be known to us through the study of the Bible.

Assist us by your Spirit in our understanding of the scriptures, that we may be led into the way of truth and be made wise unto salvation through the knowledge of you and of your Son, Jesus Christ our Lord. *Bible Society**

72

Almighty God, we thank you for the holy scriptures, in which you have revealed to us your Son Jesus Christ as the fulfilment of the law and the prophets, the promised Messiah of Israel, and the Redeemer of mankind.

Grant that we, who gratefully celebrate his advent and acknowledge him as your living Word, may walk in the light of his truth and make known the good news of his kingdom in all the world, to the glory of your name.

See also 53

Preparing for Christmas **73**

Lord God, as we prepare for Christmas may we not fail to prepare *ourselves* for this great festival.

Help us, amid all the busyness of these days, to find time to think of what Christmas really means: of your love for the world, of the coming of the promised Redeemer, of the mystery of the Word made flesh; and like Mary may we treasure up these things and ponder them in our hearts, so that we may be ready to join in the joyful worship of Christmas Day, to the glory of your name.

Frank Colquhoun

74

Father, in your mercy Christmas comes again, and in faith we set out on the road to Bethlehem to see this thing that has happened.

Lead us on our journey, and kindle in our hearts a spirit of expectancy; and may we not rest until we bow in wonder and adoration before the Child of Mary, the everlasting Son of the Father, and sing "Glory to God in the highest!"

Frank Colquhoun

75

Lord, as we make ready for Christmas amid so much affluence and abundance, keep us mindful of the poverty-stricken peoples of the world, the vast multitude who at this very time lack the bare necessities of life.

Through the gifts we offer for their relief may we show something of our gratitude for all that you have given us; and may our gifts be acceptable through him who for our sake became poor and was born in a stable, Jesus our Saviour.

Frank Colquhoun

CHRISTMAS

Praise and wonder **76**

BLESSED be God who in his love stooped to redeem mankind.
Blessed be the King who made himself poor to enrich the needy.
Blessed be the holy Child who was born of the Virgin Mary.
Blessed be the eternal Word who was made flesh for us.
Blessed be Jesus our Saviour and Lord, now and for evermore.

77

O God, who by the birth of your Son in the stable of Bethlehem made highest heaven stoop to lowest earth: give us grace so to ponder in our hearts this great and mighty wonder that we may respond with gladness to your unspeakable gift, and be raised at last from earth to heaven; through Jesus Christ our Lord. *After A. Campbell Fraser*

78

Lord, help us to approach the Christmas story
with a fresh sense of wonder as we think of Jesus:
the Son of God, yet born of Mary;
the incarnate Word, yet a child without speech;
the Lord of glory, yet a baby cradled in a manger.
Thanks be to you, O God, for your gift beyond words!

The meaning of Christmas **79**

Lord, we know the Christmas story so well.
Help us to understand it better.
Make it more real to us, so that
with Mary and Joseph we may journey in faith to Bethlehem,
with the shepherds we may hear again the good tidings of a Saviour's birth,
and with the angels we may glorify your holy name.
So give us new joy in our Christmas worship,
and fill our hearts with wonder, love and praise.

Frank Colquhoun

80

O God, whose love has been shown to us
in the birth of Jesus our Saviour,
help us this Christmas to find time
to let your love speak to us;
that we may respond to it
in trust and adoration,
and open our hearts to receive
your grace and pardon,
your joy and peace,
through Jesus Christ our Lord.

Adapted

81

We thank you, our heavenly Father, for the loveliness of the Christmas story:
the child in the manger,
the song of the angels,
the homage of the shepherds,
the tender love of Mary.
But most of all we thank you for the meaning of the Christmas story: that you loved the world so much that you

gave your only Son, that all might live through him.

All praise and thanks be yours, O God, for so great a love, so great a gift, so great a Saviour, Jesus Christ our Lord.

Frank Colquhoun

Christmas peace **82**

O Prince of Peace,
whose promised birth the angels sang
with "peace on earth":
grant peace to us all,
peace in the world,
peace in our homes,
and peace in our hearts,
this Christmastide and evermore.

Timothy Dudley-Smith

83

Give us, our Father, this Christmas time,
peace in our hearts,
that we may create peace in our homes
and help to spread peace in the world,
for Jesus Christ's sake.

The needy at Christmas **84**

Loving Father, as we thank you for the joy of Christmas, we bring to you those for whom this season is clouded by sickness or anxiety, by poverty or unemployment, by loneliness or bereavement.

Keep them from bitterness or despair as they remember the birth of him who for our sake became poor, that we might possess the true riches; and may the song of the angels find an echo in their hearts; for Jesus' sake.

Frank Colquhoun

The Christmas crib **85**

Into this holy place at this happy time, O Lord, we come to worship that little Child whose nature revealed your own and what ours might become. We ask that the lovely things in his nature may grow in us and that all things hostile to his spirit may die; for his name's sake.

Leslie D. Weatherhead

86

Holy Child of Bethlehem,
born in a stable,
laid in a manger,
no place is too low or mean
for you to enter.
Come to us this Christmas time,
dwell in our hearts and homes,
and fill them with your love,
your peace, yourself,
now and always.

Adapted

The Bidding Prayer. A modern version **87**

Good Christian friends, at this Christmas time let us prepare ourselves to hear again, in word and song, the good tidings of God's redeeming love made known to us in the birth of the Holy Child of Bethlehem; and with the angelic host let us give glory to God in the highest.

But first let us pray for the needs of the whole world: for peace and goodwill among all nations; for unity and brotherhood within the Church of Christ our Lord, especially in this town [*or* village, city] and in our diocese of . . . ; for love and harmony in our communities, our families and our homes; and for a blessing on all children dear to us, and on loved ones absent from home.

Let us also remember at this time those for whom Christmas brings little joy: the poor and homeless, the hungry and destitute, the sick and those who mourn; and all the victims of human tyranny, cruelty and oppression.

Lastly, let us remember with thanksgiving those who shared our Christmases in years gone by and who now rejoice with us in the greater light of God's heavenly kingdom. To their company, and to the fellowship of all the citizens above, may God in his mercy bring us all.

These prayers let us gather up in the words our Saviour Christ taught us:

"Our Father . . . " *Frank Colquhoun*

NEW YEAR AND EPIPHANY

The new year **88**

GRANT, O Lord, that as the years change,
we may find rest in your unchangeableness.
May we meet this new year bravely,
sure in the faith that while men come and go,
and life changes around us,
you are ever the same,
guiding us with your wisdom
and protecting us with your love;
through Jesus Christ our Lord. *After William Temple*

89

God, bless the coming year,
and give us in your mercy
time for the task,
peace for the pathway,
wisdom for the work,
and love to the last;
for Jesus' sake.

The naming of Jesus **90**

We praise you, heavenly Father,
that you gave to your incarnate Son
the name of Jesus,
for it is the name of our salvation.
May it be to us,
and to all your people,

the name that is above every name,
the name to be honoured, trusted and adored,
now and for evermore. *Frank Colquhoun*

The Epiphany **91**

Almighty God, whose Son our Saviour Jesus Christ is the light of the world: grant that we and all your people may shine with the radiance of his glory, that he may be known, worshipped, and obeyed to the ends of the earth; through Jesus Christ our Lord, who with you and the Holy Spirit lives and reigns, one God, now and for ever.

*Episcopal Church, U.S.A.**

92

Almighty God, who by the light of a star
led wise men to Jesus:
by the light of your Word lead us and all
nations to him,
the Saviour of the world;
that together we may bring him our best gifts,
and pay homage to him as our King.

93

Lord Jesus, may your light shine upon our way,
as once it guided the steps of the magi;
that we too may be led into your presence
and worship you,
the Child of Mary,
the Word of the Father,
the King of nations,
the Saviour of mankind;
to whom be glory for ever.

The baptism of Jesus **94**

Father in heaven, who at the baptism of Jesus in the River Jordan proclaimed him your beloved Son and anointed him with the Holy Spirit: grant that all who are baptized into his name may keep the covenant they have made, and boldly confess him as Lord and Saviour; who with you and the Holy Spirit lives and reigns, one God, in glory everlasting.

Episcopal Church, U.S.A.

LENT

Penitence **95**

GOD our Father, you have set forth the way of life for us in your beloved Son. We confess with shame
our slowness to learn of him,
our failure to follow him,
our reluctance to bear his cross.
Forgive, according to your steadfast love,
the poverty of our worship,
our neglect of fellowship and the means of grace,
our hesitating witness for Christ,
our imperfect stewardship of your gifts.
Have mercy upon us, O God;
cleanse us from our sins,
and put a new and right spirit within us;
for the sake of Jesus Christ our Saviour.

Adapted from the Covenant Service,
Church of South India

96

Heavenly Father, we confess how often we disobey
what we know to be your will;
how often we forget you
and leave you out of our lives;
how often we are too blind to know our sins,
too proud to admit them,
too indifferent to make amends.
We confess how half-hearted and unworthy we are
as members of your Church

and as your witnesses before men.
In your mercy, O Lord, forgive us our sins,
and give us honest, humble and penitent hearts,
for the sake of our Saviour Jesus Christ.

After William Temple

97

Son of Man, our Saviour, we remember that your sternest judgements were reserved for the religious people of your day, because they failed to live up to their profession.

Forbid it, Lord, that we, who so often and so readily take your name upon our lips, should come under the same condemnation.

Help us in this season of Lent to search our hearts and examine our lives and to have done with all hypocrisy and pretence; that we may be what we seem to be, put our creed into practice, and bear a witness that will honour you before men. *Frank Colquhoun*

98

Almighty God, lover of all men,
giver of all grace,
look mercifully upon us
who acknowledge our sins;
create in us a pure heart
and a steadfast spirit;
and lead us in the paths of
holiness and righteousness;
through Jesus Christ our Lord.

99

Father, we confess that we have sinned against you
and are no more worthy to be called your children.
Yet we believe that you love us still,

and that your love is unchanging.
Have mercy upon us, O God.
Grant us true repentance;
forgive us all that is past;
cleanse and renew our hearts;
and help us to rise victorious over every weakness
in the strength of our Saviour Jesus Christ.

Frank Colquhoun

100

O God, who sent your Son Jesus Christ
to be the Saviour of mankind:
teach us to know our sins
and to turn from them;
show us what is our duty
and help us to do it;
and so lead us by your Holy Spirit
that we may walk in the way of your will;
through Jesus Christ our Lord.

Temptation and victory **101**

Almighty God, whose blessed Son was tempted in every way as we are, yet did not sin: grant that by your Word and Spirit we may be enabled to triumph over every evil, and to live no longer for ourselves alone, but for him who died and rose again for us, Jesus Christ our Lord. *Adapted*

102

Holy Spirit of God, inspirer of all that is good and true in life, come into our hearts and fill them with your light and strength.

Help us to hate all sin and selfishness, and to fight against them with unfaltering courage and resolve; and because we are weak and cannot prevail without your help, clothe us with your power and give us the victory, through Jesus Christ our Lord. *Harold E. Evans*

Those who have gone astray **103**

O God, whose glory it is always to have mercy: be gracious to all who have gone astray from your ways, and bring them again with penitent hearts and steadfast faith to embrace and hold fast the unchangeable truth of your Word, Jesus Christ your Son; who with you and the Holy Spirit lives and reigns, one God, for ever and ever.

Episcopal Church, U.S.A.

Refreshment Sunday **104**

Gracious Father, whose blessed Son Jesus Christ came down from heaven to be the true bread which gives life to the world: evermore give us this bread, that he may live in us, and we in him; who lives and reigns with you and the Holy Spirit, one God, for ever and ever.

Episcopal Church, U.S.A.

Mothering Sunday **105**

O God, the true Mother, as well as the Father, of all men and women, from whom we come, to whose breast we return at last, we thank you this day for all good mothers [and especially for our own].

For their care and patience and love in childhood's earliest days, for the prayers they offered, the counsels they gave, the example they set, we bring you our praise; through Jesus Christ our Lord. *Leslie D. Weatherhead**

See also 338–44

PASSIONTIDE

Passion Sunday **106**

O GOD, by the Passion of your blessed Son you made an instrument of shameful death to be for us the means of life: grant us so to glory in the cross of Christ, that we may gladly suffer shame and loss for the sake of your Son our Saviour Jesus Christ; who lives and reigns with you and the Holy Spirit, one God, for ever and ever.

Episcopal Church, U.S.A.

Palm Sunday **107**

Dear Lord and Master,
you showed the world your princely power
by riding into Jerusalem on a donkey.
Grant to us all that even as we rejoice in you as our King,
we may follow you in your great humility to the cross,
and so may experience the glory of your victory over sin and death.

Alan Warren

The blessing of palms **108**

We praise you, Almighty God, for the acts of love by which you have redeemed us through your Son Jesus Christ our Lord.

On this day he entered the holy city of Jerusalem in triumph, and was proclaimed as King by those who spread their garments and branches of palm along his way.

Let these branches be for us signs of his victory; and grant that we who bear them in his name may ever hail him as our King, and follow him in the way that leads to eternal life; who lives and reigns in glory with you and the Holy Spirit, now and for ever. *Episcopal Church, U.S.A.*

Holy Week **109**

Lord Christ, who for love of our souls
chose the costliest following of the Father's will:
forgive us, who have so often followed the easy path of selfish desire,
and set your law of sacrifice within our hearts;
that we may be ready to deny ourselves
and courageously walk in your steps, our crucified Redeemer;
who lives and reigns in the glory of the Father and the Holy Spirit,
one God for evermore

Maundy Thursday **110**

Almighty Father, whose dear Son, on the night before he suffered, instituted the Sacrament of his Body and Blood: mercifully grant that we may receive it thankfully in remembrance of Jesus Christ our Lord, who in these holy mysteries gives us a pledge of eternal life; and who now lives and reigns with you and the Holy Spirit, one God, for ever and ever. *Episcopal Church, U.S.A.*

See also 442–4

111

Lord Jesus, in the olive garden you faced in prayer
the devil's last and greatest temptation:
to take the easy way, the sensible solution,
that was not the will of your Father.
Give us grace, Lord, to listen

to the quiet insistent voice
that draws us up the Calvary path,
far from the world's highway:
the path that leads to the cross,
but also to the empty tomb
and the glory of the resurrection;
for your name's sake. *John Kingsnorth*★

Good Friday **112**

It was for us, Lord Jesus, that you endured all this:
the hatred, the treachery, the rejection of men;
the scourging, the mockery, the crown of thorns;
the agony and shame and dereliction of the cross.
It was for us men and for our salvation
that you suffered and died.
Give us each one a deeper understanding
of what you have done for us,
and of what we owe to you;
that we may live as those who are no longer their own
but have been bought with a price,
the price of your life-blood, O Lamb of God,
our most gracious Redeemer and King.

Frank Colquhoun

113

We adore and magnify you, O Lord our God, that in Christ crucified you reveal the fact that the very essence of your nature is a Love that will go to the uttermost lengths for every man: for the lost, the lowest, and the least; for each and every one of us here as we kneel at the foot of the cross today. *Adapted*

114

God of infinite love,
on this day above all days
we sing the praise of him who died,
of him who died upon the cross.
We bless you for the words he uttered,
for the anguish he endured,
for the sacrifice he offered,
for the triumph he won over sin and death.
Accept our gratitude, our worship, our adoration,
and make us more worthy of all that he has done for us,
our Lord and Saviour Jesus Christ. *Frank Colquhoun*

Before meditation **115**

O God our Father, all-holy, all-loving, who gave your only Son for the salvation of mankind: look mercifully upon us your servants as we bow in penitence before his cross.

Give us faith to behold him in the mystery of his Passion, and to enter into the fellowship of his sufferings.

Let his wounds be our healing, his death our life, his shame our glory, that we may also partake of the victory of his resurrection, to the honour of your name.

Adapted

THE SEVEN WORDS FROM THE CROSS

The first word "Father, forgive them" **116**

LORD Jesus Christ,
you asked forgiveness for those who crucified you,
for they did not know what they were doing.
We acknowledge that we are often caught in the web of the world's sin;
that we fail to recognize the deceitfulness of our own hearts,
the depths of our own self-seeking;

that we crucify you afresh.
Forgive us, O Lord, all our wrong doing
against you, our neighbour, and ourselves,
and help us to forgive those who cause us hurt;
for your mercies' sake. *Llewellyn Cumings*

The second word "With me in paradise" **117**

Lord Jesus Christ,
you spoke the word of promise
to the criminal who turned to you
in the last hours of his life.
We thank you that it is never too late
to repent and to believe in you.
Reassure all who, nearing death,
acknowledge their sins
and seek your grace and forgiveness.
Have mercy on all men, O Lord,
and on us, unworthy sinners as we are,
for you are our Saviour and Redeemer.
Llewellyn Cumings

The third word "Woman, behold your son!" **118**

Lord Jesus Christ,
in your last hours of pain
you took thought for your mother
and commended her to the beloved disciple's care.
Help us, when trials overtake us,
to have thought for our loved ones
and for those in need about us.
Make us to know that we are members of your family,
and that nothing can separate us from your love;
for your name's sake. *Llewellyn Cumings*

The fourth word "My God, why have you forsaken me?" **119**

Lord Jesus Christ,
who, being made sin for us,
endured the darkness of a spiritual dereliction
that you might bring us to God:
be near to all who suffer alone
and are conscious only of pain and darkness.
In the immensity of your compassion
reveal yourself to them, O Lord,
that they may know that they are not forsaken
but are surrounded by your love;
for your tender mercies' sake. *Llewellyn Cumings*

The fifth word "I thirst" **120**

Lord Jesus Christ,
you thirsted in anguish of body and soul on the cross:
thirsting for drink;
thirsting for the accomplishing of God's work;
thirsting for the salvation of the world.
In your infinite longings for us, O Lord,
lead us to yourself, the fountain of living water,
that we may find our thirst quenched
in knowing you and doing your will,
now and for ever. *Llewellyn Cumings*

The sixth word "It is finished!" **121**

Lord Jesus Christ,
you willingly suffered on the cross
all that was necessary for our eternal salvation
and drained the cup of sacrifice to the last.
We thank you for your great work of redemption,
achieved once for all at infinite cost,

by which we are reconciled to God.
Help us to rest our faith on what you have done
and to know that the way to the Father's presence
is open to us all through the cross,
now and for evermore. *Llewellyn Cumings*

The seventh word "Father, into your hands . . ." **122**

Lord Jesus Christ,
who in the hour of death committed yourself
into your Father's hands:
be with us when the time comes
for our departure from this world.
May your grace sustain us at the end;
may we know ourselves accepted by our Father;
and may we pass peacefully into your presence,
where faith turns to sight,
where we shall see you face to face,
and we shall be for ever with the Lord.

Llewellyn Cumings

EASTER

Praise and worship **123**

THE Lord is risen! and we are risen with him
The Lord is risen! and life eternal is ours.
The Lord is risen! and death has met its master.
The Lord is risen! and the way to heaven is open.
The Lord is risen! He is risen indeed!
Alleluia! *Frank Colquhoun*

124

Almighty and eternal God, whose Son Jesus Christ
vanquished the power of sin
and rose triumphant over death:
with your whole Church in heaven and on earth
we worship and adore you;
and we ask you so to raise us up with Christ
in newness of life,
that we may serve you henceforth
in the power and joy of the resurrection
and glorify you for evermore. *Adapted*

125

Living God, our Lord and King,
we render you the tribute of our praise
for the resurrection of the springtime,
for the everlasting hopes that rise within the human heart,
and for the gospel of the resurrection
which has brought life and immortality to light.
Receive our thanksgiving,

reveal your presence,
and send forth into our hearts
the Spirit of the risen Christ.

Adapted from W. E. Orchard

126

Almighty God, who through your only Son Jesus Christ overcame death, and opened to us the gate of everlasting life: grant that we, who celebrate with joy his glorious resurrection, may be risen with him, and seek the things that are above, where he lives and reigns with you and the Holy Spirit, one God, for ever and ever.

A revision of the 1662 Easter collect

127

Be present, O risen Lord,
in this your Church's Easter praise;
that its anthems of joy
and its proclamation of your victory
may worthily celebrate
both the mystery of your redeeming love
and the majesty of your eternal glory.

C. N. R. Wallwork

128

Living Lord, vanquisher of sin and death,
come among us in your risen power
and make your presence known to us
in Word and Sacrament this Easter Day.
Speak your message of peace to our hearts;
show us your wounded hands and side;
and send us forth to your service
in the power of the Holy Spirit,
to the glory of your name.

Based on John 20. 19–23

129

We praise you, O God, for this joyful Eastertide
as we celebrate again the great redemption
won for us by our Lord Jesus Christ
and his victory over death.
Grant us by your grace to enter into his triumph,
to share his risen life,
and at last to be partakers of his endless joy,
to the glory of your holy name. *Frank Colquhoun*

130

O God our King, by the resurrection of your Son Jesus Christ on the first day of the week, you conquered sin, put death to flight, and gave us the assurance of everlasting life.

Redeem all our days by this victory; forgive our sins, banish our fears, and make us bold to praise you and to do your will; through Jesus Christ our Lord.

Episcopal Church, U.S.A.

The Easter hope 131

We thank you, Lord God, that because of Easter our gospel is not least a gospel about the mystery of death as well as of life.

May those who face death at this time, and especially those who have watched it claim their loved ones, know that through Christ's glorious resurrection death has lost its sting for ever.

He has opened the kingdom of heaven to all who believe in him. He has broken the power of death and brought life and immortality to life.

Thanks be to God who gives us the victory through our Lord Jesus Christ! *Adapted*

The Easter gospel **132**

Almighty Father, we praise you for your victorious love and power made known to us in the death and resurrection of your Son our Lord.

Help us to remember that what Christ has done for us by his Easter triumph he has done for all mankind; and make us eager to share this good news with others, that all nations may join with us in our Easter praise, to the glory of your name. *Frank Colquhoun*

The Good Shepherd **133**

O God, whose Son Jesus Christ is the good shepherd of your people: grant that when we hear his voice we may know him who calls us each by name, and follow where he leads; who, with you and the Holy Spirit, lives and reigns, one God, for ever and ever. *Episcopal Church, U.S.A.*

ASCENSIONTIDE

Adoration **134**

JESUS, our ascended and exalted Lord,
to whom has been given the name above all names:
we worship and adore you.

Jesus, King of righteousness, King of peace,
enthroned at the right hand of the Majesty on high:
we worship and adore you.

Jesus, our great High Priest, our Advocate with the Father,
who lives for ever to make intercession for us:
we worship and adore you.

Jesus, the Pioneer of our salvation,
bringing many sons to glory through your passion:
we worship and adore you.

"To him who sits on the throne and to the Lamb,
be praise and honour and glory and power,
for ever and ever!" *Frank Colquhoun*

135

We give you thanks and praise, Lord Jesus Christ,
that in your ascension you have taken our human nature to the Father's throne in heaven;
and we pray that, since as King you demand from us all that we are,
so as perfect Man you will share with us all that you are,
that we may be more nearly conformed to your image,
to the glory of your name. *Basil Naylor*

The footprints **136**

Dear Lord, at this happy and holy season help us to see that the real footprints of your ascension are to be found, not upon a mountain-top near Jerusalem, but in the marks and tokens of the witness of your disciples here and now, living and serving in the presence of their ascended Lord.

Alan Warren

Christ the King **137**

Almighty God, you have exalted your Son Jesus Christ and given him a kingdom, that all peoples and nations should serve him: make us loyal subjects of our heavenly King, that we may always hear his word, obey his commands, and further his will; and hasten the day when every knee shall bow to him and every tongue confess that he is Lord, to your eternal glory and praise. *After A. Campbell Fraser*

138

Almighty God and Father, we thank you
that the head that once was crowned with thorns
 is crowned with glory now.
We celebrate with joy the kingship of Jesus.
Give us grace to acknowledge his rule
 in our lives as well as with our lips,
and to serve his worldwide kingdom;
that the day may be hastened
when all nations shall own him Lord,
and he shall reign for ever and ever.

Frank Colquhoun

PENTECOST

The gift of the Spirit **139**

LORD Jesus, we thank you that you have fulfilled your promise and given us your Spirit to abide with us for ever: grant us to know his presence in all its divine fullness.

May the fruit of the Spirit be growing continually in our lives;

may the gifts of the Spirit be distributed among us as he wills to equip us for your service;

and may the power of the Spirit be so working in us that the world around may increasingly come to believe in you.

We ask it, Lord, in your victorious name.

Michael Botting

140

Holy Spirit of God, on the day of Pentecost
you came once for all to the Church
as the gift of the exalted Lord.
Come to us in your grace and power today,
to make Jesus real to us,
to teach us more about him,
and to deepen our faith in him;
that we may be changed into his likeness
and be his witnesses in the world,
to the glory of God the Father. *Adapted*

Mission and service **141**

O God, who to an expectant and united Church
granted at Pentecost the gift of the Holy Spirit:
give us the help of the same Spirit
in all our life and worship,
that we may expect great things from you
and attempt great things for you,
and show to the world your Son our Saviour Jesus Christ;
to whom with you and the Holy Spirit be honour and glory,
now and for evermore. *Church of South India*

142

Almighty God, who on the day of Pentecost
opened the way for the preaching of the gospel
to people of every race and nation and tongue
by the promised gift of the Holy Spirit:
renew your Church in the power of the same Spirit,
that its witness may reach to the ends of the earth,
and all flesh may see your salvation,
revealed in Jesus Christ our Lord. *Adapted*

143

O Lord our heavenly Father,
renew in us the gifts of the Holy Spirit.
Increase our faith,
strengthen our hope,
enlarge our charity;
and make us ever ready to serve you,
both in body and soul,
through Christ our Lord.

The fire of the Spirit **144**

O God, may the fire of your Holy Spirit
consume in us all that displeases you,
and kindle in our hearts a burning zeal
for the service of your kingdom;
through Jesus Christ our Lord.

Adapted from an ancient collect

The wind of the Spirit **145**

Holy Spirit of God,
all-powerful as the wind you came
to the Church on the day of Pentecost,
to quicken its life
and empower its witness.
Come to us now as the Wind of heaven
and breathe new life into our souls;
and revive your work among us,
that God in all things may be glorified,
through Jesus Christ our Lord.

Frank Colquhoun

HARVEST THANKSGIVING

Thanksgiving **146**

ALMIGHTY and gracious Father, we give you thanks for the fruits of the earth in their season and for the labours of those who harvest them.

Make us, we pray, faithful stewards of your great bounty, for the provision of our necessities and the relief of all who are in want, to the glory of your name; through Jesus Christ our Lord. *Episcopal Church, U.S.A.*

147

Almighty God, who in the beginning set man on the earth to cultivate the soil and to have dominion over created things: we give thanks today for all who work on the land and for those who market their produce and manufacture our food.

So direct and prosper their work that the fruits of the earth may be wisely cultivated, safely harvested, and generously shared; for the sake of Jesus Christ our Lord.

Llewellyn Cumings

Open-handedness **148**

Most gracious Father, you open your hands
and fill all things living with plenteousness.
As we your children partake of your bounty,
we pray that we too may be open-handed;
that we who have so freely received,
may always as freely give,

for the sake of him who gave his life for us,
our Saviour Jesus Christ.

Frank Colquhoun,
Psalm 145. 16 PBV

The earth is the Lord's **149**

"The earth is the Lord's and all that is in it."
So we sing, and so we also acknowledge.
Yet we know, Lord, that while the earth is yours,
you have appointed us stewards of your property.
Keep us faithful to our trust;
and make us mindful of our responsibility
both to conserve the earth's resources
and to distribute its benefits justly and unselfishly,
for the good of mankind, and for your great glory.

Frank Colquhoun
Psalm 24. 1

150

Almighty God, Creator and Lord of all things, we praise you for the marvels of the world you have made, for the varied beauty of earth and sky and sea, and for your provision of all things needful for our bodies.

Give us as Christians such reverence and gratitude for the created order that we may conserve and not destroy our rich inheritance, and share its bounty with the needy peoples of the world; through Jesus Christ our Lord.

The hungry world **151**

Lord of the harvest,
we rejoice in the bounty of your world;
we thank you for the rich harvests it produces.
As we do so, we remember those who do not have enough,
the thousands who are daily dying of hunger.
We pray for those who have more than they require,

for ourselves and our churches.
Show us what needs to be done,
and how to share the world's harvest more fairly.
Teach us to value people more than things.
Above all, help us to set our hearts
on your kingdom of love and justice,
and to seek to do your will here on earth,
as servants of Jesus Christ our Lord.

Adapted from Christian Aid

See also 194

Not by bread alone **152**

"Man shall not live by bread alone, but by every word that proceeds from the mouth of God."

Lord Jesus, many people have full larders,
with bread enough and to spare,
and yet inwardly they are hungry
for the things of the Spirit.
You are the Bread of Life:
without you our hearts go hungry,
our lives are empty.
Help us constantly to feed on you by faith,
that we may know the abundant life
you came to bring us all,
for the glory of your name. *Llewellyn Cumings*

VARIOUS OCCASIONS

Trinity Sunday **153**

ALMIGHTY God, you have revealed to your Church your eternal Being of glorious majesty and perfect love as one God in Trinity of Persons: give us grace to continue steadfast in the confession of this faith, and constant in our worship of you, Father, Son, and Holy Spirit; for you live and reign, one God, now and for ever.

Episcopal Church, U.S.A.

Remembrance Sunday **154**

Father of all men and lover of souls,
as on this day we hold in grateful remembrance
those who died in time of war,
we pray that the leaders of the nations
may seek your righteousness,
so that the whole world may find your peace;
through Jesus Christ our Lord. *Frank Colquhoun*

155

Lord of the nations, we remember before you with grateful hearts the men and women of our country who in the day of decision ventured their all for the liberties we now enjoy.

Help us to recognize the incalculable debt we owe them, that we may strive in our own time to maintain true freedom in our nation, and to safeguard the peace which was won at so great a cost; through Jesus Christ our Lord.

Adapted

All Saints' Day (or All Souls) **156**

Almighty God, Lord of all worlds,
we bless you for all who have entered into their rest
and reached the promised Land,
where you are seen face to face.
Give us grace to follow in their footsteps,
as they followed in the way of Christ;
and help us to see in them
the memorials of your redeeming grace,
and pledges of the heavenly might
in which the weak are made strong;
through Jesus Christ our Lord. *After F. J. A. Hort*

St. Aidan and others **157**

We thank you, O God, for all who in past centuries crossed frontiers to bring the faith to this land, especially today for your servant *Aidan*.

Grant the same vision and perseverance to those whom you call now to cross boundaries of race, colour and culture with the same faith and in the power of Jesus Christ our Lord. *John Poulton*

Commemoration of John Bunyan **158**

All praise to you, O Lord, for the grace which abounded to your servant John Bunyan, who from the riches of your Word taught us to view our Christian life as a pilgrimage from this world to that which is to come.

Give us grace to tread the pilgrim path with such true valour that we may be hindered by no discouragement; and fearing not what men say, may we labour on till at the end we inherit the life of your eternal kingdom; through Jesus Christ our Lord. *Frank Colquhoun*

St. Francis of Assisi **159**

God of all goodness and grace, who kindled a flame of sacred love in the heart of Saint Francis, so that he left all for your sake: increase in us the same power of love, that like him we may renounce the vanities of the world, befriend the poor and outcast, and delight in all your creatures; through Jesus Christ our Lord. *Adapted*

St. Hugh of Lincoln **160**

Merciful Father, who endued your servant Hugh with a wise and cheerful boldness, and enabled him to rebuke kings and princes in your name: give us grace like him not only to be bold, but to have just cause for boldness, even the fear and love of you alone; for the sake of Jesus Christ our Lord.

*W. H. Frere**

Labour Day **161**

Almighty God, you have so linked our lives one with another that all we do affects, for good or ill, all other lives: so guide us in the work we do, that we may do it not for self alone but for the common good; and, as we seek a proper return for our own labour, make us mindful of the rightful aspirations of other workers, and arouse our concern for those who are out of work; through Jesus Christ our Lord.

Episcopal Church, U.S.A.

Ember Days **162**

We make our prayer to you, O Lord our God,
for those who are to be set apart
for the work of the ordained ministry
[and especially those whom we now remember].
Grant them the abundance of your grace,
that in the power of the Holy Spirit
they may faithfully fulfil their calling

in building up the life of your Church
and in furthering your kingdom in the world;
through Jesus Christ our Lord.

163

Almighty God, who led your apostles to ordain ministers to serve in all the churches: pour out your Holy Spirit on those who are to be set apart at this time for the ministry of Word and Sacrament; that they may be strengthened for the work to which you have called them and be faithful shepherds of your flock, to the glory of your name; through Jesus Christ our Lord.

See also 410–5

IV
THE WORLD

GOD'S WORLD

The divine purpose **164**

LORD God, we live in a world where things have gone badly wrong
  because we have forgotten you
  and left you out of our reckonings.
We have worshipped other gods
  and have not hallowed your name.
We have adopted the world's standards
  and have not served your kingdom.
We have gone our own way
  and have not chosen your will.
Have mercy upon us, O Lord our God.
Forgive our sin and folly and turn us back to yourself,
  that we may worship you, the Holy One,
  submit to your kingly rule of love and justice,
  and order our lives according to your laws.
For yours is the kingdom, the power, and the glory,
for ever and ever. *Frank Colquhoun*

165

O God, loving Father of all your children,
  yet transcendent in majesty and power:
let the whole earth acknowledge your great glory
  and worship you in your holiness;
let the nations submit to your righteous rule
  and be united in a community of justice and peace;
let all men fulfil the purpose of your love

and live in obedience to your word.
So shall your name be hallowed,
your kingdom come
and your will be done,
on earth as in heaven,
through Jesus Christ our Lord. *Frank Colquhoun*

(*The above prayers are based on the first part of the Lord's Prayer.*)

Deus misereatur **166**

God, have mercy on our world, tottering on the brink of disaster and self-destruction.

Have mercy on the rulers and statesmen who bear the responsibility of ultimate decision.

Have mercy on our own nation as we face our share of responsibility.

God, have mercy on us all, and grant us your salvation; through Jesus Christ our Lord. *Frank Colquhoun*

The kingdom of God **167**

Grant us to look with your own eyes of compassion,
O merciful God, at the long travail of mankind:
the wars, the hungry millions,
the countless refugees,
the natural disasters,
the cruel and needless deaths,
men's inhumanity to one another,
the heartbreak and hopelessness of many lives.
Hasten the coming of your kingdom,
when nations shall be at peace,
free from fear and free from want,
with no more pain or tears,
in the assurance of your love

and the security of your will,
shown to us in Jesus Christ our Lord. *George Appleton*

168

Yours, Lord, is the kingdom:
yours the kingly rule of grace and truth
which changes life and makes all things new.
May your sovereignty be acknowledged
here and in all the world,
that the reign of sin may be broken,
your righteous will prevail on earth,
and the nations live together in freedom and peace.
Grant this, O God, for the sake of your Son,
Jesus Christ, our King for evermore.

Frank Colquhoun

THE NATIONS AND THEIR RULERS

Those in authority **169**

LORD God, all wise, all merciful, hear us as we pray for those who bear the responsibility of leadership among the nations of the world.

Give them in all their deliberations wisdom to know your will, regard for your laws, and respect for human rights; that they may seek to lead mankind in the paths of truth, freedom and peace, for the glory of your name; through Jesus Christ our Lord. *Adapted*

170

O God, the creator of men and nations,
  lifting up one and putting down another,
holding the earth in righteousness
  in the hollow of your hand:
have mercy upon your troubled children,
and give to this world's leaders and rulers
  a mind to seek for peace
  and the skill to find it;
through Jesus Christ our Lord.

Timothy Dudley-Smith

171

Hear us, O Lord, as we lift up before you all who bear the bewildering responsibility of government among the nations of the world.

Give them wisdom beyond their own, integrity in all their

dealings, and a resolve to seek first your kingdom and your righteousness for all mankind.

We ask it in the name of Christ.

Timothy Dudley-Smith

172

God of all mercy,
we pray for the nations of the world
in the unrest and violence of these times.
Give wisdom of mind and strength of character
to those who are called to positions of leadership;
overthrow the purposes and designs of evil men;
and establish the cause of righteousness in every land,
that all mankind may be led into the way of peace;
for the sake of Jesus Christ our Lord.

Frank Colquhoun

Nations in conference **173**

O God, ruler of the destinies of men and nations, grant to all representatives of nations who confer with one another, and to those on whose word and attitude so much depends, the guidance of your Holy Spirit and the grace of humility, that they may be ready to see a point of view which differs from their own; and keep before them not only the welfare of their own nation as they see it, but your will for the whole world; through Jesus Christ our Lord.

*Leslie D. Weatherhead**

United Nations Organization **174**

Almighty God, we pray for the leaders of the United Nations, and especially those on whom rests great responsibility at the present time.

Give them wisdom to make right decisions, courage to fulfil them, and perseverance to continue their efforts to establish peace and promote the welfare of humanity, to the glory of your name.

175

God and Father of us all, we ask your blessing on the United Nations Organization in all its manifold work:

in education and health,
in relief of poverty and hunger,
and in keeping the light of peace shining in the world.

And we pray that the leaders of the nations may be given the discernment and courage always to choose the good and refuse the evil, in obedience to your will; through Jesus Christ our Lord. *Adapted*

PEACE AND RECONCILIATION

A prayer for peace **176**

GIVE peace in our time, O Lord:
peace and reconciliation among the nations;
peace and unity within the churches;
peace and harmony in our communities and our homes;
peace and love in all our hearts;
for the sake of Jesus Christ our Saviour.

Frank Colquhoun

International peace **177**

Most merciful God, the refuge of all who put their trust in you, we turn to you with penitence and humility as we acknowledge our share in the world's sinfulness.

We turn to you with faith and hope, for you alone can save.

Break down the barriers of fear, of hostility and of misunderstanding, that divide the nations from one another; and prosper all counsels that make for sanity and charity, for a just and enduring peace; through Jesus Christ our Lord.

Adapted

178

God of all grace
and lover of all nations,
we pray for peace
in our hearts and in our homes,
in our nation and in the world,

the peace of your will,
the peace of our need;
in the name of Christ our Lord.

179

Look mercifully, O Lord our God,
upon the world of our day,
and heal the sorrows and sufferings of mankind.
Save the nations from the lust of power,
from racial hatred and jealousy,
from the worship of material things;
and grant that in every land
the rule of tyranny may be broken,
the cause of righteousness may triumph,
and all peoples may learn to serve you
in the peace and freedom of your kingdom;
through Jesus Christ our Lord. *Frank Colquhoun*

180

Almighty God, whose will it is that all nations should live in harmony and understanding with one another: so lead us that we may put justice and freedom before our own selfish needs, and by seeking to be good citizens of this kingdom may help forward the coming of your kingdom of love and peace in the world; through Jesus Christ our Lord.

*Prayers for the City of God**

181

O God, we bring before you the deep divisions of our world. Set in men's hearts the spirit of penitence, forgiveness, and reconciliation, that they may no longer distrust or fear one another, but be drawn together in understanding; so that in unity of purpose they may seek the way of peace; through Jesus Christ our Lord.

182

Merciful Father, hear the prayers of all who cry to you for help at this time, that mankind may be saved from the horror and tragedy of war; and grant that the nations of the world, recognizing the needs and rights of one another, may seek the costly way of reconciliation, in accordance with your will; through Jesus Christ our Lord. *Frank Colquhoun*

183

Heavenly Father, be with us in our search for peace,
in ourselves and in the world you have made.
Diminish pride and increase humility;
weaken suspicion and nourish trust.
Deepen true love and understanding in every heart,
and unite us all in the bonds of brotherhood
as members of one family;
through Jesus Christ our Lord. *Adapted*

184

Lord God, remove fear, prejudice and hatred
from the hearts of all people,
for these are the things that make for war.
Replace them with trust, understanding and compassion,
which are the things that make for peace.
We ask in the name of the Prince of Peace,
Jesus Christ our Lord. *Anglican Pacifist Fellowship*

Peace in the Near East **185**

Lord and Creator of all the ends of the earth, we pray for peace among the children of Abraham.

Where Jew and Moslem and Christian are oppressed by their history and their hate, restrain the wicked and strengthen the peace-makers.

Where there are signs of hope and beginnings of understanding, grant perseverance.

Make us aware, beyond the defeats and despairs we bring upon ourselves, of your aching heart of love for all peoples, our one God and our Judge. *John Poulton*

Racial harmony **186**

Lord Christ, you are our peace, for by your cross you have broken down the dividing wall of hostility between the races.

By the power of your Spirit reconcile us to the Father and to our brothers and sisters of every colour and culture; that we may be no longer strangers to one another, but fellow citizens with the saints in the household of God, for the glory of your name. *Based on Ephesians 2. 14–19*

187

Lord Jesus Christ, by whose cross all enmity is ended and all walls of separation are broken down: look with compassion on the racial antagonisms of your world; and make us by your grace agents of reconciliation where there are divisions of colour or class among men; for you are our peace, now and for ever.

The human family **188**

Heavenly Father, who made us in your image and redeemed us through Jesus your Son: look with compassion on the whole human family.

Take from us the arrogance and hatred which infect our hearts; break down the walls that separate us; and unite us in bonds of trust and understanding, that we may work together to accomplish your purposes on earth, for the glory of your name; through Jesus Christ our Lord.

Episcopal Church, U.S.A.

TODAY'S WORLD

World poverty **189**

FATHER, we who live in the midst of affluence confess that much of the world's poverty is caused by our selfishness and our indifference to the suffering of our fellow men.

Teach us to remember that the good things of this life are given to us not only to enjoy but to use and to share; and help us to exercise our stewardship more faithfully and generously as we think of the needs of others; for the sake of Jesus Christ our Lord.

190

Lord of the nations and friend of the poor,
strengthen in the leaders of today's world
  a belief in human dignity and in basic human rights;
  a belief in the values of justice, freedom and peace,
  in love and generosity,
  in reason rather than force.
So may the nations grow in mutual respect and understanding,
and recognize that the problem of world poverty
is the concern and responsibility of them all.
Grant it for Christ's sake.

Based on words in the Brandt Report

191

O God, the Father of all mankind,
have mercy on us and all your children.
Forgive us for the mess we have made of your world:

for the selfishness of nations,
for the waste of natural resources,
for the injustices done by the powerful to the powerless,
for our disobedience to your way of love made known to us in Jesus Christ.
Make us instruments of your will, and give us
the humility to admit our wrong doing,
the courage to stand for what is right,
the determination to fight for the poor and oppressed,
and the faith to believe that with you all things are possible;
through Jesus Christ our Lord.

Adapted from Christian Aid

192

God our Father, we thank you for your compassion and care for all your children.

Give us a deeper understanding of the needs of our suffering brothers and sisters in the world, and implant in our hearts your love of justice, truth and mercy.

Transform our complacency into concern, and our concern into action; and accept the service we offer in partnership with our fellow Christians in other lands, as together we walk in the footsteps of your Son, Jesus Christ our Lord.

Adapted from Christian Aid

193

Holy Father, we confess how often we have lived in selfishness, and done little or nothing to help others in their need.

We confess our indifference to the sorrows and sufferings of the world.

Touch our hearts with deeper sympathy and compassion; and give us an active concern to right the wrongs, to heal the wounds and to restore the broken relationships of men; for the sake of Christ our Lord.

British Council of Churches

The hungry **194**

Most merciful God, we commend to your care the men, women and children of our world who are suffering anxiety and distress through lack of food.

Strengthen and support them in their need; and grant that the nations may grow in their concern for one another and in their readiness to share all your gifts; that all may live together in the fellowship, freedom and joy of your kingdom; through Jesus Christ our Lord.

*Morning, Noon and Night**

See also 151

Richer and poorer nations **195**

O God, your Son taught us that from those to whom much has been given, much will be required.

Grant wisdom and political courage to the leaders of the richer nations of the world.

Forgive past selfishness and present complacency.

Strengthen their resolve to find fairer ways of international commerce, and surer paths to peace.

So may all your children live together justly, and walk humbly with you; through Jesus Christ our Lord.

John Poulton

Conservation **196**

O God our heavenly Father, you have blessed us and given us dominion over all the earth: increase our reverence for the mystery of life; and give us new insights into your purposes for the human race, and new wisdom and determination in making provision for its future in accordance with your will; through Jesus Christ our Lord.

Episcopal Church, U.S.A.

197

O God, the only source of life and energy and wealth,
defend our planet earth.
Teach us to conserve and not to squander the riches of nature,
to use aright the heritage of former generations,
and to plan for the welfare of children's children.
Renew our wonder, awaken our concern,
and make us better stewards and more careful tenants
of the world you lend us as our home.
Hear us, O Lord, our creator and redeemer,
in the name of Christ.

Timothy Dudley-Smith

198

Almighty God, in giving us dominion over all things on earth, you made us fellow workers in your creation.

Give us wisdom and reverence so to use the resources of nature, that no one may suffer from our abuse of them, and that generations yet to come may continue to praise you for your bounty; through Jesus Christ our Lord.

Episcopal Church, U.S.A.

Scientific research **199**

Lord God, you have revealed to this generation wonders and mysteries of your universe hitherto unknown.

Forgive us because we have often turned our larger knowledge to foolish and cruel uses, and filled the world with terror and anguish.

Increase in all of us the power to dwell in peace together, and to settle our disputes without resort to violence, that we may be able to put away the instruments of war, and use your gifts to save life, not to destroy it; through Jesus Christ our Lord. *Episcopal Church, U.S.A.*

200

O God, whose wisdom has set within our hearts
the quest for knowledge and dominion in the natural world,
teach us to use all science, invention and technology
not to hurt but to heal,
not to destroy but to build,
not to divide but to unite your human family in
prosperity and dignity together.
And let not our knowledge outstrip our wisdom;
through Jesus Christ our Lord.

Timothy Dudley-Smith

201

God of all wisdom, enlighten the minds of men of science who search out the secrets of your creation; that their humility before nature may be matched by their reverence towards you.

Save us from misusing the results of their work, that the forces they set free may enrich the life of mankind, and that your name may be hallowed both in the search for truth and in the use of power; through our Lord and Saviour Jesus Christ.

V
OUR NATION AND SOCIETY

THE NATION

The nation's spiritual needs **202**

LORD God of our fathers, we thank you for your mercy towards our nation throughout its long history.

Hear us as we seek your continuing mercy in this our day.

Deliver us from the sins of affluence, from pride, from materialism, and from indifference to the needs of the developing world.

Inspire your Church to be the nation's conscience.

Give to our leaders soundness of judgment and courage of decision; and unite us all in a common zeal to honour you and serve mankind; through Jesus Christ our Lord.

J. R. W. Stott

203

Most merciful God, we ask for our nation
  not material prosperity
  or a higher standard of living,
but what is most for its true welfare:
  a renewal of Christian faith,
  a recovery of spiritual values,
  a return to the paths of righteousness;
and this we pray in the name of Christ our Lord.

Frank Colquhoun

National unity **204**

Lord God Almighty, you have made all the peoples of the earth for your glory, to serve you in freedom and peace: give to the people of our country a zeal for justice and the strength of forbearance, that we may use our liberty in the service of your kingdom and for the furtherance of your gracious will; through Jesus Christ our Lord.

Episcopal Church, U.S.A.

205

O God, we pray that your holy and life-giving Spirit may so move the hearts of the people of this land, that barriers which divide us may crumble, suspicions disappear, and hatreds cease; and grant that our divisions being healed, we may live in justice and peace; through Jesus Christ our Lord.

Episcopal Church, U.S.A.

206

Lord, you have warned us that a kingdom divided against itself cannot stand: hear us as we pray for the healing of divisions in the life of our nation.

Help us to recognize that the things we have in common are of greater worth than those on which we differ.

Deepen our understanding of one another's needs and our respect for one another's opinions; and unite us in the common cause of justice, truth and freedom, for the honour and glory of your name. *Frank Colquhoun*

National policy **207**

Teach us, O Lord, to see every question of national policy
in the light of the teaching of Jesus Christ;
that we may check in ourselves and in others
every temper that makes for war,
all ungenerous judgments,
all promptings of selfishness;
that being ready always to recognize
the needs and hopes of other peoples,
we may with patience do whatever in us lies

to remove suspicions and misunderstandings,
and to honour all men in Jesus Christ our Lord.

Administration of justice **208**

Lord God, the judge of all mankind, we pray for those who are called to minister justice between man and man, to clear the innocent, and to convict and punish the guilty.

Give them prudence and discernment, that without fear or favour they may justly and mercifully fulfil their duties as in your sight, to the good of our nation and the glory of your name. *Adapted*

Law and order **209**

O God, the King of righteousness, we bring to you in prayer those who bear responsibility for maintaining law and order in our land, especially judges, magistrates, and the police; that the innocent may be protected, evil doers be brought to account, the rights of all be defended, and that we as a nation may enjoy the blessing of a just and free and peaceful society; through Jesus Christ our Lord.

Frank Colquhoun

Northern Ireland **210**

Lord of the nations and lover of all men, be the guide of those in authority who today and tomorrow bear responsibility towards Northern Ireland.

Shield them from the temptations of easy speech, and from intolerance and party strife.

Sustain them with patience and courage, and enable them to make hope a possibility; that they may win men and women to a new endeavour after peace and order in that troubled land; through Jesus Christ our Lord.

211

Father, we pray for Northern Ireland,
its politicians and its people:
for the imagination and the will
so to seek reconciliation and justice
as to find stable government and peace.
Grant that as the Holy Spirit worked at first,
breaking down the dividing wall
between Jew and Gentile,
creating one new humanity in Christ,
so by the same Spirit Protestants and Catholics
may find in Christ the freedom
to share with one another,
and to care for each other in his name.

The armed forces **212**

To your care and protection, O Lord of hosts, we commend the men and women of our armed forces at home and overseas.

Defend them in the hour of danger; strengthen them in the fulfilment of their duty; and enable them to serve their country with loyalty, courage and honour; through Jesus Christ our Lord. *Adapted*

Our enemies **213**

O God, the Father of all, whose Son commanded us to love our enemies: lead them and us from prejudice to truth; deliver them and us from hatred, cruelty, and revenge; and in your good time enable us all to stand reconciled before you; through Jesus Christ our Lord.

Episcopal Church, U.S.A.

LEADERS OF THE NATION

Our Queen and nation **214**

ACCEPT our gratitude, O Lord, for the example of the Royal House, for the happy homelife established at the heart of the Commonwealth.

God save the Queen, all who are dear to her and all who advise her.

Cleanse our national life, and raise up leaders for our land who shall be beyond pettiness and self-seeking, and who shall make our Commonwealth the instrument of your will among the nations; through Jesus Christ our Lord.

Leslie D. Weatherhead

Those in authority **215**

O Lord our governor, bless the leaders of our land, that we may be a people at peace among ourselves and a blessing to other nations of the earth.

To our Queen and Government and all in administrative authority, grant wisdom and foresight in the exercise of their duties, that they may provide for the needs of all our people, and fulfil our obligations to the community of nations.

Teach us all as citizens of this country to rely on your strength and to accept our responsibilities to one another, that we may serve you faithfully in our generation and honour your holy name; through Jesus Christ our Lord.

Adapted

216

O God, your rule extends over all the earth, yet you have committed authority to the leaders of the nations.

Grant to the Prime Minister, and all members of the Cabinet, insight, compassion and courage effectively to meet the demands of these days.

To all Members of Parliament give wisdom and humility in taking counsel together, that their decisions may promote the well-being of the nation and more nearly express your will; through Jesus Christ our Lord. *John Poulton*

217

We remember before you, O God, those who exercise authority among us and influence public opinion in Church and State, in industry and commerce; all who speak to the nation through broadcasting and the press; and all who have power over the lives of others.

Grant them the humility to seek your guidance and the courage to do your will, so that more people may be led to the knowledge of you and to the service of your kingdom; through Jesus Christ our Lord.

Mothers' Union Service Book

Parliament **218**

Almighty God, we pray for those engaged in the political life of our nation as Members of Parliament.

Help them to put loyalty to what is right above loyalty to party or class, above popularity or the praise of men; and may their only motive be to serve their country and promote the welfare of their fellow men.

We ask this for the honour of your holy name.

219

Almighty God, whose counsels are perfect
in wisdom and love:
we remember before you those who serve in Parliament;
and that they may order the life of the nation
in the right way, help them
to love mercy,
to do justly,
and to walk humbly before you;
for the sake of Jesus Christ our Lord. *Llewellyn Cumings*

220

Eternal God and Father, from whom comes every good and perfect gift, we pray for those entrusted with the responsibility of government in this land.

Endue them with the spirit of wisdom, and keep them in your fear; that in obedience to your laws they may promote the well-being of the nation, and further the cause of justice and peace in the world; through Jesus Christ our Lord.

Adapted

Our economic ills **221**

O Christ, whose righteous anger fell once on those who set the honour of your Father's house below their private gain:

raise up among us men and women of skill and courage, to lead our nation from fear and greed towards justice and peace, from deprivation and want towards dignity and opportunity, from the injustices that divide us towards fairness and equity.

And what here we pray for, teach us truly to desire; through Jesus Christ our Lord. *Timothy Dudley-Smith*

A general election **222**

Direct, O Lord our God, the minds of the citizens of this country in the election of those to represent them in the high court of Parliament; that the nation may be wisely governed, the rights of all may be protected, and your Church may be free to serve and witness in obedience to your word; through Jesus Christ our Lord. *Adapted*

223

Lord God, in your mercy raise up as candidates for Parliament men and women who love truth more than power, and their country more than themselves.

Give electors insight to distinguish between sound policy and party propaganda; and so direct the issues of this election that we may be blessed with wise leaders, good government, and just laws; through Christ our Lord. *Adapted*

IN TIME OF CRISIS OR UNREST

Tension and conflict **224**

O GOD, you have bound us together as a nation in a common life: help us, amid the tension and unrest of these times, to confront one another without hatred or bitterness, and to work together with mutual forbearance and respect for the cause of justice and truth; through Jesus Christ our Lord. *Adapted*

225

God and Father of us all,
hear the prayer we offer for our nation
in this time of tension and strife.
Forgive the misery we bring upon ourselves
through disobeying your laws
and selfishly ignoring the needs of others.
Save us from the disruptive forces among us.
Strengthen all who are working on the side of justice.
And unite us as a people in the love of freedom
and in the cause of righteousness;
for Christ our Saviour's sake. *Frank Colquhoun*

The inner cities **226**

Hear our prayer, Lord, for all whose lives are impoverished and beset by the problems of our inner cities.

Guide those in local and central government, the planners, the administrators, the decision-makers; and may they see the welfare of its citizens as the city's highest good.

Raise up in such areas men and women of integrity and energy as leaders, ministers and teachers; in industry and commerce, in health and social services, in the police and in all the work of community and industrial relations.

And this we ask for Jesus Christ's sake.

Timothy Dudley-Smith

227

Our Father, we pray for the homes and families and for the children of the inner cities; for those whose families are broken, for the badly housed, the lonely and the handicapped, and for all whose lives seem purposeless or who cannot find work.

We remember especially young people growing up amid urban deprivation and decay.

Give to us all the will to seek for them a better quality of life, true opportunity, a future and a hope.

In the name of him who loved Jerusalem, and wept for it, even Jesus Christ our Lord. *Timothy Dudley-Smith*

228

Merciful Father, we bring to you in our prayers the people of our inner cities: their frustration in failing to find work and a meaningful purpose in life, and their sense of being neglected, deprived, and unwanted.

Direct the minds of those whose policies control their lives;

give vision and understanding to those appointed to serve their welfare;

and stir our consciences to recognize their claims upon our sympathy and generosity;

that men, women and children in our inner cities may find the way to the happy fulfilment of their lives; through Jesus Christ our Lord. *Basil Naylor*

229

O Lord our God, we pray for all who administer or live in our cities.

In a time of violence, help the police and magistrates to be just in their actions and effectively to maintain the peace.

In a time of tension, help the press and the media to be accurate in their reporting, and to encourage decisions based on truth.

In a time of national depression, help both Government and Opposition to be sober and sensitive in their public utterance, and effectively to act for the common good; through Jesus Christ our Lord. *John Poulton*

Christians in troubled areas **230**

Lord Jesus Christ, who taught us to fear nothing but only him who can hurt the soul, we pray for Christians working in perilous places.

Prosper their work; uphold them in danger; use them as peace-makers in their service of others; and garrison their hearts and minds with the knowledge that in life or in death you are with them, their Saviour now and for ever.

John Poulton

In time of disaster **231**

Lord, we pray not only for those whose homes have been darkened by disaster in recent days, but also for those whose faith has been shaken; for those who stand bewildered and fearful in the midst of tragedy; for the injured, the bereaved, and the destitute.

We commend to your grace all who are seeking to help and heal the injured, and to comfort and calm the bereaved.

From you alone can come the word that will lift them above their darkness. Answer, O Lord, the question in men's minds; and assure them that though disaster is not of your will, you are present with them in their suffering and sorrow, and can enable them to find purpose, hope and peace again.

Stanley Pritchard

232

Most merciful God, in the midst of natural disaster
we look to you in hope and trust,
acknowledging that there is much in life
beyond our present understanding.
Accept our compassion for the suffering;
bless those who are working for their relief;
and show us what we can do to share in their task,
as servants of Jesus Christ our Lord.

*Morning, Noon and Night**

THE LIFE OF SOCIETY

Money and possessions **233**

GUARD us, O Lord, from the wrong use of money:
 from selfishness, carelessness, or waste;
and from that obsessive love of money
 which is a root of all evils.
Enable us to be good stewards
 of what is entrusted to us;
to give or spend or save according to your will;
so that neither poverty nor wealth
 may hinder our discipleship,
 harm our neighbours,
 or destroy our life;
through Jesus Christ our Lord. *Christopher Idle*

234

Help us, O Lord, to understand the place of money in our life.

Keep before us the peril of loving it.

Help us to make it our servant, never our master.

And let neither the lack of it, nor the possession of it, loosen our grasp upon the true riches, which are ours through the grace of Jesus Christ our Lord.

Dick Williams

235

Lord Christ, you have taught us that our life does not consist in the abundance of our possessions.

Write this word on all our hearts today.

Save us from the sin of covetousness, from the love of money, from the materialistic spirit of the age.

Help us to set our affections on the things of eternal worth, the things that money cannot buy; that we may lay up treasure in heaven, and may know that even now, in possessing you, we possess the true riches.

Frank Colquhoun

Television **236**

O God, you sent your Son among us
to be the Way, the Truth, and the Life:
help those who are responsible for television
to use their creative gifts humbly and responsibly;
acknowledging their influence on where people choose to go,
on what they choose to believe,
and on the style of life they choose to follow;
through Jesus Christ our Lord.

John Poulton

237

Lord God, you have placed in human hands great power for good or evil through television.

We pray for those whose faces and voices are thus known in millions of homes; for those who decide policies and plan schedules; and those who direct and produce programmes.

We pray that their skills and gifts may be devoted to what is true and good, so that those who watch and listen may be informed and entertained without being debased or corrupted; through Jesus Christ our Lord.

Christopher Idle

Writers and broadcasters **238**

O God, who chose the written word to speak an eternal gospel to every age, give to those who handle words as writers, speakers, journalists and broadcasters a constant loyalty to truth and a heart concerned with wisdom.

May they raise, and not lower, our moral standards, and increase, not diminish, the true welfare of mankind; for the sake of Jesus Christ our Lord. *Timothy Dudley-Smith*

239

Heavenly Father, who through your Son warned us that by our words we shall be justified or condemned: we pray for writers, journalists and broadcasters whose words so powerfully influence the life of the nation.

Help them to recognize in the words they write or speak a power for good or for evil, and to use them responsibly as those who must give an account; through Christ our Lord.

Llewellyn Cumings

Music and musicians **240**

Most merciful Father, who so created man that in music he might voice that which is beyond speech: we praise you for the music makers of every race and nation, and for the instruments of music which men have fashioned for their use.

And we pray that as by music we are brought to share together in a richer life, so we may praise you in a fuller dedication to your service; through Jesus Christ our Lord.

Adapted

Partnership in service **241**

O God, in whose providence we are closely bound together in the bundle of life, help us to remember how much our lives depend upon the courage and industry, the honesty and integrity, of our fellow men and women.

May we be mindful of their needs, grateful for their services, and faithful ourselves in our responsibilities towards them; for Jesus Christ's sake.

*Reinhold Niebuhr**

Those who serve the community **242**

God our Father, we remember before you with gratitude those who in their different capacities serve the community.

We pray for those who safeguard the public health and minister to the sick;

those who provide for the welfare of the young and care for the elderly and infirm;

those who serve in local government, administer the law, and preserve the peace.

Assist them in their varied duties, and deepen within us all the spirit of loving service; through Jesus Christ our Lord.

Frank Colquhoun

Local government **243**

Almighty God, we pray for those who exercise authority in government, and especially in this place where we live.

Grant that they may be upright in character and wise in judgment, seeking first and foremost the good of the community, not their own advantage; and so direct and strengthen them in all their work and planning that they may further your will among us, for the glory of your name.

Adapted

Public health **244**

Lord God, from whose creative power all health and healing flows, we thank you for medical knowledge and skill, and for every advance in the care of those who are ill or injured or in pain.

Teach us so to order our society as to place a true value upon the health of all; and so to care for others that medical resources may be more fairly shared among the peoples of the world; to the glory of your name.

Timothy Dudley-Smith

The world of business **245**

We pray, O God, for those whose lives are immersed day by day in the busy and complex world of commerce, with its many demands, responsibilities, and temptations.

Save them from being so absorbed in material wealth that they lose sight of the things of priceless value, the things that are worth more than all the money in the world.

Give them integrity of character, that their lives may be sincere, their dealings honest, and their words truthful; we ask it in the name of Christ, the Lord of all life.

Frank Colquhoun

Those whose work is dangerous **246**

Eternal Father, strong to save, we pray for those whose work is often dangerous and on whom the lives of others so largely depend:

for the members of the armed forces, the police, and the fire brigades;

for coastguards and those who man the lifeboats;

for the crews of helicopters engaged in rescue service.

Uphold them, O God, in the fulfilment of their duties, and protect them in every peril of land and sea and air; we ask it in the name of Christ our Lord. *Frank Colquhoun*

Fishermen **247**

Lord, be with those who go down to the sea in ships,
and who know the cost of fish in terms of human lives.
Be with them when the tempest is beyond their seamanship,
when the skill of captain and crew is of no avail.
Be with them when the harvest of the sea is poor,
and they must risk everything to get a living.
Be with them in sickness, disablement, and bereavement.
Be with the Royal National Mission to Deep Sea Fishermen
in all its caring work for fishermen and their families.
Lord, be the Pilot and Saviour of our fisher-folk.
Enfold them in the net of your love,
and bring them to safe haven.

Stanley Pritchard

Seafarers **248**

Lord and heavenly Father, we commend to your keeping all who sail the seas.

Guard them in danger; protect them in temptation; sustain them in loneliness; and support them in sickness and anxiety.

Bless all who minister to their bodily and spiritual needs; and guide us all to the haven of eternal life; through Jesus Christ our Lord.

Missions to Seamen

Users of the road **249**

God our Father, hear us as we pray for protection and safety when we travel by car.

Teach us respect for the law and for the rights of other road users.

Help us to put our Christian faith into practice in the way we drive, to set a good example to others, and to give you thanks when we arrive safely at our destination.

Adapted

A road-user's prayer **250**

Help me, O God, as I drive,
to love my neighbour as myself,
that I may do nothing to hurt or endanger
any of your children.
Give to my eyes clear vision,
and skill to my hands and feet.
Make me tranquil in mind
and relaxed in body.
Deliver me from the spirit of rivalry,
and from resentment at the actions of others;
and bring me safe to my journey's end,
for Jesus Christ's sake. *Vyvyan Watts-Jones*

INDUSTRY

Work **251**

O GOD, the creator of all things, who made us in your own image so that we should seek joy in creative work, we give thanks for your creation and for those whose work brings joy to others.

We pray for those who find their work hard and dull, and for those who are unemployed.

Help us to order our public life so that everyone may have the opportunity to work, and may find satisfaction in doing it; through Christ our Lord.

Industrial relations **252**

As we pray, Creator God, for the complex world of industry, we remember the delicate balance of relationships, the heavy responsibility of management, the often monotonous and repetitive job-assignments, and the ever-present fear of redundancy and unemployment.

We pray that harmony may reign in the industrial areas of our land, and that the creative skills with which you have endowed mankind may be employed to your glory and the well-being of society.

We pray this in the name of Jesus Christ our Lord.

Michael Botting

253

Almighty God, whose Son Jesus Christ
  served at the carpenter's shop:
grant to those engaged in our industrial life
  the spirit of service and a sense of duty;

and give to the leaders of industry
  understanding of the workers' needs,
that in the settling of all disputes
  justice, honour and goodwill may prevail,
to the glory of your name. *Frank Colquhoun*

254

We thank you, our Father, for those who in years past worked hard to win justice and a fair wage for workers in industry.

We pray that in these better times in which we live we may be given fresh understanding of others' needs and a genuine concern for their welfare.

Save us all from folly, greed and self-seeking; and grant that both management and labour may accept the need for change, and may plan to meet it and make it together.

Industrial disputes **255**

Lord of all life, we pray for those involved in the present industrial disputes:

for those who make claims and those who must accept or reject them;

that both parties may be ready to listen rather than to oppose, to respect rather than to suspect one another;

and that from their meeting together may come what is right for all concerned and for the good of the nation; through Jesus Christ our Lord. *Basil Naylor*

256

O God, whose purposes are just and true
  and whose will is peace:
grant that in all our divisions,
  and in this present industrial unrest,
truth may be honoured, justice be done,

and lasting peace prevail;
through Jesus Christ our Lord.

Timothy Dudley-Smith

Unemployment and redundancy **257**

Lord Christ, you said to your disciples, "My Father has worked till now, and I work": we pray for those who through no fault of their own have been deprived of the work that leads towards the fulfilment of their lives.

Inspire and guide those who bear the responsibility of finding the answer to our industrial problems.

Open their minds to the truth, that they may discern in the events of our time the direction of your will; and give them the courage to declare what they believe to be right, and the power to carry it through. *Basil Naylor*

258

Heavenly Father, give wisdom to the leaders of our nation as they seek to resolve the problem of unemployment and to secure productive work for all.

Help the churches to minister to the unemployed in their areas and to provide them with voluntary work wherever possible; and enable each of us to be sensitive to their needs, and to be ready when necessary to make sacrifices for the sake of others, as servants of Jesus Christ our Lord.

Michael Botting

Night workers **259**

O God, your unfailing providence sustains the world we live in and the life we live: watch over those, both night and day, who work while others sleep; and grant that we may never forget that our common life depends upon each other's toil; through Jesus Christ our Lord.

Episcopal Church, U.S.A.

EDUCATION

Schools and colleges **260**

ETERNAL God, bless all schools, colleges and universities and especially . . . , that they may be lively centres for sound learning, new discovery, and the pursuit of wisdom; and grant that those who teach and those who learn may find you to be the source of all truth; through Jesus Christ our Lord. *Episcopal Church, U.S.A.*

261

God of love, inspire by your Spirit all those involved in the work of our schools.

Bless pupils and parents, teachers and governors, caretakers and cleaners, secretaries and supervisors, committee members and administrators.

Grant that, working together for the common good, they may make their schools places where real learning may take place and where all may discover the true meaning of life; through Jesus Christ our Lord. *Maurice Burrell*

262

O God of truth, we pray for all places of education, and especially for this *college*:

for its council and officers, that they may be guided aright in their plans and decisions;

for the members of the teaching staff, that their varied talents and skills may be dedicated to your service;

for the students, that they may accept with gratitude and

humility their gifts of mind and the opportunities to use them;

for the chaplain(s) and all who share in the work of pastoral care and spiritual oversight.

These prayers we offer, O God, in the name of Jesus Christ our Lord. *Basil Naylor*

A school assembly **263**

We bring before you, Almighty Father,
  the life of this our school.
Grant us throughout this day
  vitality of mind,
  ability of body,
  and charity of heart.
Show us the satisfaction of serving one another,
and of building cheerfully together a school
which will be the best that we can offer in your
  service;
for the sake of Jesus Christ our Lord.

Timothy Dudley-Smith

Teachers **264**

Father, we pray for those who teach in our schools, especially in the schools of this *town*.

Give them a true sense of vocation, that they may regard their work not as a job to be done or a means of earning their living, but as a service to be rendered to children and young people in your name, and for your glory; through Jesus Christ our Lord. *Adapted*

265

God of truth and love, we remember before you those who train the minds of our children.

May they grip the imagination of those whom they teach,

and encourage children to think and judge for themselves.

And may our children learn how to send their roots down into the soil of life's enduring values, that they may grow up healthy and strong in body, mind and spirit; for the sake of Christ our Lord. *Stanley Pritchard*

266

Jesus, Lord and Master, who came to bear witness to the truth and to teach us the way of life: send your blessing on those engaged in the work of teaching.

Give them clearness of vision and freshness of thought, that they may wisely train the hearts and minds of the children committed to their care, and so prepare them to fulfil their appointed place in the life of the world; through Jesus Christ our Lord.

267

We thank you, O Lord, for those who devote their lives to the work of education in our schools and colleges.

May they do their work in humble dependence on your grace; and may it be their constant endeavour not only to impart knowledge but to build character, and to equip the young people they teach with a firm faith, a courageous spirit, and a true sense of values; for Jesus Christ's sake.

Frank Colquhoun

Learners **268**

We thank you, heavenly Father, for all that we have gained through education.

We thank you for new knowledge, new skills, new

experiences, new pleasures, and new insights.

Help us, we pray, to continue to learn all through our lives.

Give us the determination never to be content with less than the best.

Above all, grant that we may find in Jesus the more abundant life which he came to give, and which he promises to all who put their trust in him; for his name's sake.

Maurice Burrell

269

Lord Jesus Christ, you have called us to be your disciples.
Deliver us from the pride of thinking
we have learnt all we need to know,
done all we need to do,
and become all we need to be.
As we remember that disciples are learners,
enable us continually to learn as we follow you;
for your name's sake.

Maurice Burrell

Students **270**

God our Father, giver of all wisdom, we pray for students at college and university who are preparing for their work in the world.

Help them to discover both their potential and their limitations; to seek your guidance and fulfil your purpose for their lives; and to employ the gifts you have given them in the service of others, and for your glory; through Jesus Christ our Lord.

Adapted

Overseas students **271**

Heavenly Father, to whom all are dear, we pray for those who come to this country from other parts of the world to study in our colleges and universities.

Help them to make the most of their opportunities, and to find friends among those with whom they stay; and may they return to their homeland not only equipped for useful careers, but also filled with the desire to promote international understanding and goodwill; through Jesus Christ our Lord. *Adapted*

VI
HUMAN NEED AND SUFFERING

THE SANCTITY OF LIFE

Reverence for life **272**

ETERNAL Father, source of life and light,
 whose love extends to all people,
 all creatures, all things:
grant us that reverence for life
 which becomes those who believe in you,
lest we despise it, degrade it,
 or come callously to destroy it.
Rather let us save it, secure it,
 and sanctify it,
after the example of your Son,
 Jesus Christ our Lord. *Robert Runcie*

273

Lord God Almighty, our Creator,
as we gather in your presence
we celebrate our existence,
 we rejoice to be alive.
Teach us to understand more and more profoundly
that every human life is sacred,
whether it belongs to an unborn infant
 or to a terminally ill patient;
to a handicapped child
 or to a disabled adult;
to people who live next door
 or to those who live far away.

Remind us, heavenly Father, that each individual
has been made in your image and likeness
and has been redeemed by Christ.
Help us to see each other with your eyes,
so that we may reverence, preserve and sustain your gift of life in them,
and use our own lives more faithfully in your service.
We ask this through Christ our Lord. *Basil Hume*

274

Almighty and ever gracious God,
at whose word man was given life,
by whose Son Jesus Christ man finds new birth
and the promise of eternal life:
teach us to reverence all that you have made
by offering ourselves as the temple of the Holy Spirit,
by protecting and promoting all that is gracious and good,
by opposing all ideas and practices that would degrade or destroy life.
To this ministry we commit ourselves,
through Jesus Christ our Lord. *Andrew B. Doig*

The medical profession **275**

Lord God, the giver of life, may it be the constant aim of all members of the medical profession to preserve life as well as to heal sickness and alleviate suffering.

Help them, and all of us, to face the challenge of secular humanist thinking and to take a clear stand for Christian values, and to affirm our conviction that life is sacred from conception to the grave.

This we ask in the name of Christ our Lord.

Adapted

The unborn child **276**

Lord Jesus, whose holy mother was told by the message of an angel that the fruit of her womb would be blessed: we pray for all mothers who are awaiting the birth of a child.

May they follow the example of your mother, and know that all life created by you is holy.

Keep them in your peace, guard them from harm, and grant them the fulfilment of their joy; for your name's sake.

*W. Temple Bourne**

Doctors and nurses **277**

SANCTIFY, O Lord, those whom you have called to the study and practice of the arts of healing, and to the prevention of disease and pain. Strengthen them by your life-giving Spirit, that by their ministries the health of the community may be promoted and your creation glorified; through Jesus Christ our Lord.

Episcopal Church, U.S.A.

278

We thank you, our Father, for those whose lives
are dedicated to the healing of the sick
and to the relief of suffering;
and we ask your blessing upon their work
in our hospitals, nursing homes and clinics.
We pray also for those engaged in medical research,
that cures may be found for those diseases and disorders
at present beyond man's skill and aid.
Of your mercy hear us, O God,
as we pray in the name of Jesus our Lord.

Frank Colquhoun

279

Lord Jesus Christ, the great physician, to whom in days of old the sick and suffering were brought that you might make them whole: let your healing work be done today through the knowledge and skill of doctors, surgeons and nurses, especially in the hospitals of this *town*; that those who suffer from disorders of body or mind may be restored to fullness of health, for the glory of your great name. *Adapted*

280

Heavenly Father, we know that all healing comes from you, and therefore we ask your blessing on all who are engaged in the ministry of healing.

We pray for doctors, surgeons, and psychiatrists,
for health visitors and district nurses,
for the staff who work in our local hospitals,
and for those who nurse the sick at home.

Give them, O Lord, all needful wisdom, skill and patience; and may they know that in ministering to the sick they are fellow workers with you and are furthering your purposes of love; through Jesus Christ our Lord. *Adapted*

The Red Cross Society **281**

Almighty God, source of all strength and understanding, make us fearless and constant in upholding the ideals of the Red Cross.

Inspire us anew with the spirit of sympathy and self-sacrifice, that we may be compassionate in our care of the sick and suffering; and grant that in promoting the health and welfare of the peoples of our own and other lands we may help to foster international friendship and goodwill; through Jesus Christ our Lord.

The Church's ministry of healing **282**

Bless, O Lord God, your Church in its ministry to the sick, that it may fulfil your holy will and purpose, and use all means of grace for the healing of your people; and grant to those who desire your healing true penitence, full pardon, and perfect peace; for your dear Son's sake, Jesus Christ our Lord. *Guild of St Raphael**

Prayer at the laying on of hands **283**

In the name of God most high
may release from your pain be given you
and your health be restored according to his will.
In the name of Jesus Christ, the Prince of life,
may new life surge through your mortal body.
In the name of God the Holy Spirit,
may you receive inward health
and the peace that passes understanding.
And may God, who gives us peace, make you completely his,
and keep your whole being, spirit and soul and body,
free from all fault at the coming of our Lord Jesus Christ.

Guild of Health

At the anointing with holy oil **284**

Outwardly and with sacramental oil
your body has received anointing.
So may Almighty God, our Father,
inwardly anoint your soul,
to strengthen you with all the comfort and joy
of his most Holy Spirit.
Through the power of Jesus Christ our Lord
may you be loosed from all that troubles you
in body, mind, or spirit,
to praise the Blessed Trinity, one God,
beyond all time and space, eternally.

Guild of Health

THE SICK, DISABLED AND HANDICAPPED

The sick **285**

WE bring to you, O loving Saviour, those sufferers of whom we think and whom we name in the silence of our hearts . . .

All healing is with you. We can only bring them to you and offer our minds in love and tenderness and sincerity.

Grant them healing, if that may be; but above all, grant them your peace and joy that they may know that you are with them, that they are safe, and that nothing can snatch them from your hand or finally defeat your purposes.

We ask it for your name's sake. *Leslie D. Weatherhead*

286

O God of love and power, we come to you for those who are ill in body or mind, and for those who are cast down and sad.

Tell them in the midst of all their pain and anxiety that your name is Love; and since you have ordained that your own will needs our co-operation, use these our prayers.

Turn our caring into their courage, our solicitude into their succour, our faith into their will to get well; through Jesus Christ our Lord. *Leslie D. Weatherhead*

287

Heavenly Father, we commend to your love and care
those who suffer in body, mind, or spirit,
  and especially those known to us
  whom we hold up to you in silence now.
In your goodness and mercy grant them

health of body,
soundness of mind,
and peace of heart,
that in wholeness of being they may glorify your name, through Jesus Christ our Lord. *Frank Colquhoun*

288

We are in the presence of God our Father.

We bring into his presence, in the name of the Lord Jesus, those for whom we pray.

Our prayer for them and for ourselves is that we may come to know his love more surely, to trust him more deeply, and to realize the presence of the Holy Spirit within us all, ever at work healing, strengthening, and guiding us in all our ways. *Guild of Health**

289

Lord Jesus Christ, you healed many who were blind and lame and suffering from many kinds of illness.

We believe your healing power is as great as ever.

We bring to you those whom we have named, that they may receive comfort and hope and recovery of health.

Take our thoughts and prayers and use them to further your work of healing today, for your name's sake.

The dying **290**

Most merciful Father, in whom we live and move and have our being, grant to your servants grace to desire only your good and perfect will; that whether living or dying they may know themselves to be yours, now and for ever, in Jesus Christ our Lord. *Adapted*

See also 512–3

The mentally ill **291**

Heavenly Father, we remember to our comfort that you have in your special care all broken, outworn, and imperfect minds.

Give to those who live with them the understanding and loving Spirit of Christ;

enlighten those who are tempted to laugh at such illness or regard it with shame;

and to all who are separated in this life by barriers of mind, grant the peace and consolation of your Holy Spirit; through Jesus Christ our Lord. *Guild of St Raphael*★

292

God of all grace, we bring to you in our prayers those who are passing through the darkness of mental illness, or suffering from deep depression of spirit.

Give sympathy, patience and gentleness to those who minister to their needs and to those dear to them who share the strain of their illness; and make known your healing love and power, for the sake of Jesus Christ our Lord.

Frank Colquhoun

A mental hospital **293**

Saviour of men, who of old healed those who were sick in mind as well as in body: reach forth your loving care to those in this hospital; and though their minds may be darkened or distorted, speak to their hearts your word of peace; for your tender mercy's sake. *Henry Cooper*

The handicapped **294**

O God, the Father of the helpless, we pray for handicapped people and all who suffer from any kind of disability.

Give them fresh courage to face each day, and the comfort

of the knowledge that you love and care for them.

Open our eyes and touch our hearts, that we may be sensitive to their needs and do all that we can to help them; for Jesus Christ's sake. *Mothers' Union Prayer Book*

The deaf **295**

God of all mercy, speak to our hearts, that your word may awaken in us a deeper concern for the needs of those who are handicapped by deafness.

May they be delivered from the loneliness of silence, and find within it the fullness of your love; and may they know the melody of the Spirit in their hearts, through the grace of Jesus Christ our Lord. *Adapted*

Deaf and dumb **296**

Heavenly Father, whose Son Jesus Christ opened the ears of the deaf and the lips of the dumb: we commend to your compassion those who today lack powers of hearing and of speech; that by faith they may hear plainly the voice of your love, and sing your praises joyfully in their lives, to the glory of your name. *After E. Milner-White*

PEOPLE IN NEED

The suffering **297**

ETERNAL God, whose son Jesus Christ bore our griefs and carried our sorrows, and still comes to us in the guise of the needy: hear us as we pray for those in distress:

the hungry and the homeless;
the incapacitated and the handicapped;
the mentally afflicted and depressed;
the sick and the dying;
the aged, the lonely, and the bereaved.

Help us, O Lord, who offer these prayers, to take the sufferings of others upon ourselves, and so by your grace to become the agents of your transforming love; through Jesus Christ our Lord. *Adapted*

298

Heavenly Father, whose Son taught us
that what we do for the least of his brethren
we do for him:
help us to see him and serve him
in the suffering peoples of the world,
and to love them for his sake,
who first loved us,
our Saviour Jesus Christ.

299

Father of all mercies, we pray for those in need,
and especially for those known to us:

for the sick in body or mind, that through your healing power they may be made whole;
for the disabled and handicapped, that they may have faith and courage to overcome their disabilities;
for the elderly and infirm, that they may renew their strength as they rest on your love;
and for the dying, that they may know your peace, now and at the last.
This we ask through Jesus Christ our Lord.

300

Father, we bring to you the needs of those whose lives are shadowed by suffering, praying especially for those whose sickness has no cure, whose sadness finds no comfort, and whose loneliness can never be filled.

Bind up their wounds, O Lord, and lift their hearts to you as now in silence we remember them in Jesus' name.

Victims of addiction **301**

Loving Father, who sent your Son to set men free: we pray for those who are bound by the chains of addiction to drugs, to drink, to gambling, or any other evil.

Strengthen them by your Holy Spirit, that their bonds being broken, they may be restored to fullness of life in Christ; and show us the ways by which we may both help those who suffer and prevent others from becoming enslaved. *Mothers' Union Service Book*

302

Blessed Lord, who ministered to all who came to you: we commend to your compassion those who through addiction have lost their health and freedom.

Give them the assurance of your unfailing mercy; remove

from them the fears that beset them; help them in the work of their recovery; and to those who care for them give patient understanding and persevering love, for your name's sake.

Episcopal Church, U.S.A.

303

We rejoice, heavenly Father, in the promise that in your Son Jesus Christ there is perfect freedom.

In his name we pray for those who are subject to the slavery of sin, by gambling and betting, by excessive drinking, by addiction to drugs, and by the misuse of their sexual instincts.

Enable them by the power of your Spirit to overcome these evil compulsions, and in your mercy grant them the liberty you offer them in abundance through Jesus Christ our Lord.

Michael Botting

The aged **304**

Look with mercy, O God our Father, on those whose increasing years bring them weakness, distress, or isolation.

Provide for them homes of dignity and peace; give them understanding helpers, and the willingness to accept help; and, as their strength diminishes, increase their faith and their assurance of your love.

This we ask in the name of Jesus Christ our Lord.

Episcopal Church, U.S.A.

305

Lord Jesus Christ, you are the same
  yesterday, today and for ever,
and you have promised to be with us
  all our days.
We pray for all elderly people,

especially those who are ill or housebound.
In their weakness may they find your strength,
and in their loneliness know the joy of your presence.
Be to them a sure and certain hope
of the life you have prepared for them in heaven.

Mothers' Union Prayer Book

See also 504–6

The depressed **306**

Have compassion, O Lord, on those who are depressed and cast down in spirit.

Let your light shine into their darkness.

Rekindle in them the lamp of hope.

Give them the assurance of your unchanging love and unfailing companionship; and so grant them courage to face life bravely, in the name and strength of Jesus Christ our Saviour. *Martin Parsons*

307

God of all comfort, we commend to you those who, because of their lot, are tempted to lose heart:
those who have no security of home or work;
those who see no purpose or meaning in life;
those who find it difficult to believe in you;
those who suffer from incurable illness.

Enable them to trust you, though your way is hidden from their sight, and give them courage, hope and peace in the knowledge of your love, for Jesus Christ's sake.

The underprivileged **308**

Almighty Father, as we pray for the impoverished people of the earth, help us to remember that we ourselves are poor in spirit when, in our plenty, we leave them in misery and want.

Teach us that there can be no peace in the world without justice, and no justice unless we share what we have with those who are dying of hunger.

Open our hearts to give as well as to pray, and to give generously, as we remember the example of him who gave his all for us, Jesus Christ our Lord. *Adapted*

The poor and neglected **309**

Most merciful Father, we remember before you
those whom it would be easy for us to forget:
  the poor and the homeless,
  the old and the friendless,
  and all who have none to care for them.
Bless those who minister to their needs,
that they may bring them comfort and hope;
and show us what we can do,
  as servants of your Son,
who for our sake became poor,
  Jesus Christ our Lord. *Episcopal Church, U.S.A.*

Victims of violence **310**

We commend to your merciful care, O God, those who suffer and those who sorrow as a result of acts of terrorism.

Heal the injured; comfort the bereaved; console the dying.

Deliver us from evil, and lead us all in the ways of justice and peace; for the sake of Jesus Christ our Lord.

Prisoners **311**

God of all grace, we pray with the psalmist that the sorrowful sighing of the prisoners may come before you.

Visit them with your mercy. Comfort them in the lonely, dark and bitter hours. Set them free in spirit to turn to you and find the love that forgives and welcomes us all; and so help them to face the future with new hope and courage; through Jesus Christ our Lord. *Adapted*

312

Son of God, Saviour of mankind, remember in your mercy those who have offended against the law and are serving sentences in our prisons.

Make known to them your unchanging love; turn their hearts to yourself in true repentance and simple trust; and give renewal of hope and the opportunity of making a fresh beginning; for your name's sake.

Those who suffer for the sake of conscience **313**

O God our Father, whose Son forgave his enemies while he was suffering shame and death: strengthen those who suffer for the sake of conscience.

When they are accused, save them from speaking in hate;
when they are rejected, save them from bitterness;
when they are imprisoned, save them from despair;
and to us your servants give grace to respect their witness and to discern the truth; for the sake of Jesus Christ, our merciful and righteous judge.

Episcopal Church, U.S.A.

314

Almighty God, whose Son came to preach deliverance to the captives: turn the minds of the leaders of the nations, that they may release all prisoners who suffer unjustly for their religious or political convictions; and give them a deeper understanding of the laws of your kingdom, that your will may be done on earth; through Jesus Christ our Lord.

THE SORROWFUL

For the comfortless **315**

ENFOLD, O Lord, within your loving-kindness
all those who feel rejected, unwanted, or alone.
Hear our prayer for prisoners
and all who are caught up in processes of law;
for those enclosed within a private world of desolation
by incapacity of mind or body,
by age or grief or sickness,
or because society has passed them by.
Draw near and comfort them wherever they may be;
and move the hearts of us and all your people
to care more deeply for the pains of others;
in the name of Jesus, the Man of Sorrows.

Timothy Dudley-Smith

The bereaved **316**

Grant, O Lord, to all who are bereaved the spirit of faith and courage, that they may have the strength to meet the days to come with steadfastness and patience; not sorrowing as those without hope, but in thankful remembrance of your great goodness, and in the joyful expectation of eternal life with those they love. And this we ask in the name of Jesus Christ our Saviour. *Episcopal Church, U.S.A.*

317

Almighty God, look with pity upon the sorrows of your servants for whom we pray. Remember them, Lord, in mercy; nourish them with patience; comfort them with a sense of your goodness; lift up your countenance upon them; and give them peace; through Jesus Christ our Lord.

Episcopal Church, U.S.A.

318

Heavenly Father, you know the secrets of life and death.
You know the sorrows of our hearts at this time.
Give us your comfort and peace,
and help us to trust you for the future;
that we may face every new circumstance of life
with courage, patience and hope,
in the faith of Jesus Christ our Lord. *Adapted*

319

Lord Jesus Christ, whose heart was moved to tears at the grave of Lazarus: look with compassion on your servants in this time of their sorrow and loss.

Strengthen in them the gift of faith, and may the light of hope shine within their hearts; that they may live as one day to be united again in the kingdom of your love; for your tender mercies' sake. *Adapted*

320

Heavenly Father, we lift up our hearts to you in hope and trust as we pray for those who mourn.

May they be content to release their loved one to you, assured that *he* is safe in your keeping.

Help them to believe that death is a gateway to what cannot be a lesser life.

Spare us all from the selfishness of living in the past and the luxury of private grief; and teach us to live out our lives with others and for others, till the day when we all meet in the presence of your glory; through Jesus Christ our Lord.

321

O God of love,
you gave your only Son to sorrow for our sins
and to die for our redemption:
look upon the distress of those who mourn
and ease the pain of their loss.
Out of bitterness bring the sweetness
of the knowledge of Jesus Christ,
and out of darkness
the light of true faith in him,
their Saviour and their Friend.

Michael Perry

See also 514–6

VII
MARRIAGE, FAMILY AND FRIENDS

MARRIAGE

God's will concerning marriage **322**

HEAVENLY Father, we know that marriage is of your ordaining, and that your Son blessed by his presence the wedding at Cana in Galilee.

But we also learn from his example and teaching that marriage is not your will for everyone.

Grant to each one of us the knowledge of your will, the grace to accept it, and the power of your Spirit to obey it; for in your will alone we find true peace and fulfilment.

We ask it in Jesus' name. *Michael Botting*

Engaged couples **323**

Lord Jesus Christ, who by your presence and power brought joy to the wedding at Cana: bless those engaged to be married, that there may be truth at the beginning of their lives together, unselfishness all the way, and perseverance to the end.

May their hopes be realised and their love for each other deepen and grow, that through them your name may be glorified. *Mothers' Union Service Book*

At the publication of banns **324**

Heavenly Father, bless these your servants who are to be joined together in Christian marriage.

Prepare them by your grace for the life they are to share together, and may they abide in your love and peace all their days; for the sake of Jesus Christ our Lord.

Martin Parsons

Christian marriage **325**

God our Father, who made men and women to live together in families: we pray that marriage may be held in honour; that husbands and wives may live faithfully together, according to their vows; and that the members of every family may grow in mutual love and understanding, in courtesy and kindness, so that they may bear one another's burdens and so fulfil the law of Christ; for his name's sake.

Mothers' Union Service Book

326

We thank you, God our Father,
for the joys of Christian marriage:
for the physical pleasure of bodily union,
the rich experience of mutual companionship and family life,
and the spiritual ecstasy of knowing and serving Christ together.
Help us to respond to your goodness
by recognizing you as the head of our home,
submitting to one another out of reverence for Christ,
bringing up our children in faith and godly fear,
and offering hospitality to the homeless.
We ask this in the name of Jesus our Lord.

Michael Botting

Those newly married **327**

Almighty God, giver of life and love, bless *N.* and *N.* Grant them wisdom and devotion in the ordering of their common life, that each may be to the other a strength in need, a counsellor in perplexity, a comfort in sorrow, and a companion in joy.

And so knit their wills together in your will, and their spirits in your Spirit, that they may live together in love and peace all the days of their life; through Jesus Christ our Lord.

Episcopal Church, U.S.A.

328

The God of heaven so join you now, that you may be glad of one another all your lives; and when he who has joined you shall separate you, may he again establish you with the assurance that he has but borrowed one of you for a time, to make both more perfect in the resurrection; through Jesus Christ our Lord.

329

God of love, from whom comes every good and perfect gift, bless *N.* and *N.* whom you have joined together in marriage.

May their home be radiant with joy and peace, and may all that is good and pure grow within its walls.

Give them wisdom for the daily affairs of life; bless them in time to come in the ordering of their family; and keep them in their going out and in their coming in; through Jesus Christ our Lord. *Adapted*

Marriage rededication **330**

Heavenly Father, as we look back on our married life
we want to confess our failings and mistakes,
but most of all to praise and glorify you
for all the blessings we have received.
We thank you for giving us to each other
  to have and to hold,
  for better, for worse,
  for richer, for poorer,
  in sickness and in health;
and now we rededicate ourselves and renew our vows
to love, comfort, and honour one another,
  till death us do part;
in the name of Jesus Christ our Lord.

Blessing of a civil marriage **331**

Almighty God, Lord of all life and giver of all joy, grant that *N.* and *N.* may in simple trust commit themselves to your keeping, and by your grace may live together in mutual love and faithfulness throughout their married life; through Jesus Christ our Lord.

332

Almighty Father, whose mercy is everlasting,
accept and sanctify the love of *N.* and *N.* as here,
  in your presence,
they pledge their troth one to the other
and kneel before you in penitence and gratitude,
  in trust and hope.
Keep them faithful to the vows they have made;

deepen their love and strengthen their faith;
and may your blessing rest upon them,
the blessing of the Father, Son, and Holy Spirit,
now and for evermore. *Frank Colquhoun*

Celibates **333**

Father, we remember those who stand outside the warm companionship of marriage and family: those who have chosen a lonely road, not by chance but from dedication.

We honour them, and ask a blessing on their life and witness; for by their devotion and self-giving they enrich the Church and the world, and in their love we see a reflection of your love for us all, in Jesus Christ our Lord.

Stanley Pritchard

The Mothers' Union Prayer (1974) **334**

Almighty God, our heavenly Father, who gave marriage to be a source of blessing to mankind, we thank you for the joys of family life.

Pour upon us your Holy Spirit, that we may truly love and serve you.

Bless all who are married and every parent and child. May we know your presence and peace in our homes; fill them with your love and use them for your glory.

Bless the members of the Mothers' Union throughout the world, unite us in prayer and worship, in love and service, that strengthened by your grace we may seek to do your will; through Jesus Christ our Lord.

Thanksgiving for the Mothers' Union **335**

Accept our praise and thanksgiving, O God our Father, for the faith and vision given to your servant Mary Sumner in the founding of the Mothers' Union; for its growth and development through the century past, for its world-wide fellowship of love and service, and for its witness to the things of abiding worth in marriage and family life.

Help us, who have entered into this rich heritage, to be faithful in our own day, and by your grace to build strong Christian homes and a just order of society for the generations to come; through Jesus Christ our Lord.

Frank Colquhoun
Written for the Mothers' Union centenary

See also 488–91

HOME AND FAMILY

The blessing of a home **336**

HEAVENLY Father, whose Son made his home among us here on earth: help us to recognize his presence in this home of ours which we now dedicate to your service.

Let love abound within its walls.

Grant that in every activity we may have the seal of your approval.

May all who visit us here find a haven of joy and peace; and may this our home be a foretaste of the eternal home which our Lord Jesus has gone to prepare for us, where we shall be with him for evermore. *Martin Parsons*

337

Most gracious Father,
this is our home:
let your peace rest upon it.
Let love abide here,
  love of one another,
  love of mankind,
  love of life itself,
  and love of God.
Let us remember
that as many hands build a house,
so many hearts make a home.

Hugh Blackburne

Our homes and families

338

Lord Jesus Christ, who by your coming to us in great humility sanctified the life of the home: we commend to you our homes and the members of our families, near and far.

Unite us in your love, and guard us by your power from all danger and evil.

Make us thankful for all the blessings of family life; and keep us mindful of those for whom home has no meaning; for your mercy's sake.

339

O God, whose Son prepared to save the world by sharing the life of an earthly home: help us as a family to love and serve you as we care for one another's needs; and give us those blessings which will enable us to make our home more worthy of your presence; through Jesus Christ our Lord.

*F. W. Street**

340

Father of all, who made known your love to mankind by the birth of the Holy Child at Bethlehem: help us to welcome him in our homes and to make room for him in our lives, so that we may care for one another and live at peace with all your family here on earth; through Jesus Christ our Lord.

Mothers' Union Service Book

341

God our Father, whose Son Jesus Christ
  lived at Nazareth
  as a member of a human family:
hear our prayer for all homes and families,
  and especially for our own,

that they may be blessed by his presence
and united in his love.
We ask this in his name. *James M. Todd*

342

Lord and heavenly Father, we thank you for our homes and families.

Make us aware of your loving care of us day by day.

Make us thankful for all the blessings we receive which we take for granted.

And make us mindful of those who are lonely and less fortunate than ourselves; for the sake of Christ our Lord.

Adapted

343

Heavenly Father, whose Son Jesus Christ,
born of a woman,
sanctified childhood and shared the life
of an earthly home:
bless the homes and families of our nation.
Give to parents a true sense of responsibility
in the care and training of their children;
that our boys and girls may grow up
in the fear of your name
and the fellowship of your Church,
for the glory of Christ our Lord. *Frank Colquhoun*

344

To your mercy and care, O God of love, we commit all who are dear to us, and especially those within our family circle.

Guard their lives; guide their steps; give them peace; and unite us all in your faith and fear, for the sake of Jesus Christ our Lord.

Absent members of the family **345**

Heavenly Father, you are present everywhere
and care for all your children:
we commend to you the members of our families
who are now parted from us.
Watch over them and protect them from all harm;
surround them and us with your love;
and bring us all at last to that home
where partings are no more;
through Jesus Christ our Lord. *F. W. Street*

One-parent families **346**

Loving Father, we ask you to bless fathers and mothers who are alone in bringing up their families.

Guide and strengthen them when they are beset by doubts and difficulties; help them to lead their children to know and love you; and assure them of your presence at all times; for Jesus Christ's sake. *Mothers' Union Prayer Book**

CHILDREN

The gift of a child **347**

HEAVENLY Father, creator and giver of life, there is much joy in our hearts at the news of a baby's birth, a most special and complete gift of your love, a new being and a wonder of creation.

Be with the mother and father of this little baby in their happiness, and accept their praise and ours as we give thanks to you through Jesus Christ our Lord.

*Mothers' Union Prayer Book**

See also 492–3

Godparents **348**

God and Father of us all, we pray for those who have undertaken the responsibility of serving as godparents.

Help them by your grace to fulfil their duties, and keep them faithful in prayer; that their godchildren may grow up in the knowledge of your love and in the faith of our Lord Jesus Christ, to serve and worship you all their days in the fellowship of the Church, to the glory of your name.

Adapted

Our children **349**

Father, we bring our children to you for your blessing.
Help us to be sensitive to their needs.
Give us wisdom in our care of them, that they may grow up
rooted in love,
steadfast in faith,
strong and courageous in life.

Guide us and all who have the care of children.
May we never hinder but help and encourage them
towards independence and maturity,
and to a living faith in your Son, Jesus Christ our Lord.

*Mothers' Union Prayer Book**

350

God our Father, be near to our children growing up in the peril and confusion of these times.

Guard them from the forces of evil at work in our society, and lead them in the paths of goodness and truth; and enable us as parents to give them at all times the security of our love, and the help of our example and our prayers; through Jesus Christ our Lord. *Adapted*

351

Heavenly Father, we pray for our children in their life at home and at school.

Watch over them and protect them from evil; guide them into the ways of your will; and prepare them for the work to which you are calling them in the life of the world; for the sake of Jesus Christ our Lord. *Llewellyn Cumings*

352

God our Father, we ask your blessing
on all children dear to us
and those for whom we have responsibility.
Grant that they may grow up
healthy and strong, wise and good,
in the knowledge of your love
and in the service of your Son,
Jesus Christ our Lord. *Frank Colquhoun*

353

Our heavenly Father,
your Son delighted in the happiness of children.
Bless our children and the children of our affection.
In all things protect and guide their lives;
and as they enjoy the world of your gifts,
grant them the grace of gratitude to you, the Giver;
through Jesus Christ our Lord. *Michael Perry*

Children in need **354**

O God, whose Son Jesus Christ took the children into his arms and blessed them: hear our prayer for those children who are suffering through the sin, cruelty, and stupidity of men and women.

Wipe out from their souls the stain and misery of fear, and give back to them the trustfulness and untroubled joy that should be theirs.

To those who look after them and teach them, grant faith that you are able to do this, and patient wisdom to co-operate with you; for the sake of Jesus Christ our Lord.

355

God our Father, we commend to your compassion children in need:

those whose bodies are handicapped by injury or illness;
those whose minds are retarded;
and those whose lives are warped by broken marriages and unhappy homes.

Enable all who care for them to minister with tenderness and understanding; and give them the assurance of your unfailing love; through Christ our Lord. *Adapted*

356

Lord Christ, Saviour of mankind, by your coming to the world as a helpless child move the hearts of men and women today to care for children born in poverty, or suffering from malnutrition, or dying for lack of medical aid.

Bless all who work to bring them the help and relief they need; and show us what you would have us to do, as those who profess your name and call you Lord.

Children at risk **357**

Heavenly Father, we pray for children in all kinds of danger: on the roads; from the stranger offering sweets; from the unseen and often unknown cruelty of men and women.

Give us the courage to speak out against all that may corrupt their minds or injure their bodies.

Show us, with your wisdom, how to warn them without frightening them, and help us to assure them of your presence with them everywhere; through Jesus Christ our Lord. *Mothers' Union Prayer Book**

Unwanted children **358**

Father, we remember before you unwanted babies: those whose very birth is a reminder of a love that did not last, a bitterness to the memory, a mortgage on freedom.

Be with those who take such little ones to their hearts, who make a home for them, and surround them with the love that is their lost birthright.

May such children pass untarnished through their early years, so that no mark of the past may stain the brightness of their future, and life for them may become an enriching heritage.

We ask it in Christ's name. *Stanley Pritchard*

FRIENDSHIP

Our friends **359**

HEAVENLY Father, we thank you for our friends, and especially those who have shared our troubles and sorrows in times past and have supported us in life's dark valleys.

Help us to value our friends and to regard each one as a gift and token of your love. And make us ready to extend friendship to others around us and to remember the lonely, the housebound, and those who need a friend's helping hand; for Jesus Christ's sake. *Frank Colquhoun*

360

May the God of all love,
who is the source of our affection
for each other formed here,
take our friendships into his keeping,
that they may continue and increase
throughout life and beyond it,
in Jesus Christ our Lord. *William Temple*

361

Father, as we now remember our friends before you
and ask your blessing upon them,
we thank you for all that they give to us
in affection and companionship,
in counsel and spiritual support.
Help us on our part to give to them
as generously and unselfishly in return,
and always to count our friends
as among the richest blessings of this life;
through Jesus Christ our Lord. *Frank Colquhoun*

Absent friends **362**

Lord Christ, our unseen yet eternal friend and the guardian of our love, we pray for our friends and loved ones now parted from us.

Bless them with the fullness of your grace and power; and keep us, O Lord, so near to yourself that we may evermore be near to each other.

If it is your will, give us the renewal of our fellowship on earth; and grant us at last our perfect union in the friendship of the Father's house. *Harold E. Evans**

The friendless **363**

Father, we bring to you in prayer
people whose lives are starved of friendship:
those who find it difficult to make friends;
those who are cut off from their friends by distance;
and those who in old age have lost the friends they had.
Comfort and sustain them, O Lord, with your love.
Help them to discover new interests in life
and to seek fellowship in the family of the Church.

Above all, may they find a friend in Jesus
and daily enjoy his companionship.
We ask it in his name. *Adapted*

Special friends **364**

Lord, I thank you for my special friends:
those with whom I share secrets and private names;
those who know my moods and yet still offer their affection and understanding;
those to whom I can unburden the weakness of my nature, and who can strengthen me against myself;
those who delight in my successes, and encourage me to rise again from my failures.
Lord, for these special friends I pray.
May I keep such friendships in good repair.
May I never forget them or dishonour them.
May they and I, together, be held within the circle of your love. *Stanley Pritchard*

VIII
THE CHURCH UNIVERSAL

THE CHURCH'S LIFE AND WITNESS

Spiritual renewal **365**

LORD Jesus Christ, grant renewal to us your people,
and grant renewal to your whole Church:
renewal of love for you and for one another;
renewal of faith in your promises and in the power of the gospel;
renewal of vision for the work of your kingdom throughout the world.
Renew our lives, O Christ, after your own image.
Renew us by your indwelling Holy Spirit,
and make us strong for service and witness,
in your name and for your glory.

Frank Colquhoun

366

Renew your Church, O God,
for mission and service,
and make it here and everywhere
a living fellowship of the Spirit,
revealing your love to the world,
reconciling men to you and one another,
and serving all who are in need,
for the glory of Christ our Lord.

367

Lord, help your Church to be the Church,
the Church as you would have it be,
loyal to its Lord and faithful to its calling.

Lord, save your Church from compromise and self-interest:
from accommodating itself to the false values of the world;
from substituting a comfortable religion for an adventurous faith;
from being absorbed in its own concerns and neglecting its world mission.

Lord, have mercy on your Church.
Cleanse it, revive it, enlighten it, empower it;
and what we thus ask for all your people,
we ask also for ourselves,
in the name of Jesus Christ our Saviour.

Frank Colquhoun

368

Grant that your Church, O God,
here and in every place,
may offer a living worship to you in your glory,
and a living witness to the world in its need;
through Jesus Christ our Lord. *Frank Colquhoun*

The Church in a particular country **369**

Eternal God and Father, lover of all men and giver of all grace, bless the people of . . . and guide them along the paths of your will.

To your Church in that land give faithfulness, to her leaders wisdom and courage, to all her members patience and love; that they may boldly confess the faith of Christ crucified and be united in a fellowship of love and service; for the glory of your name. *Adapted*

370

Heavenly Father, we thank you for the witness of your Church throughout the world, as we pray now especially for the Church in . . .

Give to her leaders
discernment in their ministry,
compassion for all who are in need,
courage to stand for what is right and true,
and boldness to proclaim the gospel to those they serve.

Grant this for Jesus Christ's sake

The Church in this land **371**

Grant your blessing, O God, to your Church in this land, and prosper our endeavours to make our nation one in which your name is known and honoured.

May increasing numbers hear and receive the good news of your love and saving power;

may Christian standards triumph in public and in private life;

and may your kingly rule be extended throughout our society; through Jesus Christ our Lord. *Adapted*

372

Most merciful Father, we bring to you the spiritual needs of our country.

Revive your work among us, and inspire your Church to greater faithfulness and renewed zeal in your service.

May your continued blessing rest on all efforts to make known the good news of your Son Jesus Christ, that many may be turned to you in repentance and faith and may know the joy of your salvation.

Grant this, O God, for your glory and for Christ's sake.

The suffering Church **373**

Be merciful, O Father of all mercies, to your Church throughout the world, that all your faithful people may have grace to confess your holy name; and especially be merciful to those who are under persecution for their testimony and their profession of the gospel; that as they stand fast for your holy word, so they may be upheld by it, through your Son our Saviour Jesus Christ. *Church Missionary Society*

374

We pray, O God, that you will protect our fellow Christians who suffer imprisonment, banishment or torture because of their witness to truth and righteousness in the service of your kingdom.

Too often, we confess, we ourselves accept uncritically the status quo and are contented beneficiaries of an unjust world order.

Help us to dedicate ourselves anew to the struggle to secure justice and freedom for all people and nations, that the kingdoms of this world may become your kingdom, and Christ may be all in all. *John Kingsnorth*

375

Lord Jesus Christ, you were tempted in all points as we are, yet remained steadfast and loyal to the Father's will: hear us as we remember our fellow Christians in all parts of the world whose faith is being tested today:

those suffering persecution or imprisonment for the gospel's sake;

those who are withstanding the antagonism and ridicule of unbelievers;

and all who are tempted to turn back because the way is hard.

Give them, O Lord, the courage and patience to endure; uphold and strengthen their faith; and may their witness be the means of drawing others to you as their Saviour; for your name's sake. *Adapted*

Religious communities **376**

Lord Christ, who for our sake became poor,
give your grace to those who at your call,
and after your example,
have left possessions, parents, and hope of family,
that they might take up the cross and follow you
in the way of poverty, chastity, and obedience;
that through the consecration of their lives,
and the power of their prayers,
your Church may be renewed in holiness
and more nearly conformed to your image,
for the glory of your name. *Adapted*

377

Lord, you have undertaken to repay many times over your servants who give up brothers or sisters, father, mother or children, land or houses, for the sake of your name.

We praise you for all who have followed your saints in the ways of poverty and simplicity [especially *N* and *N*].

Bless their communities, their worship and their service; increase the number of those who heed your call to join them; granting them in this life the fulfilling of your promises, and in the world to come life everlasting.

John Poulton

The Church and social justice **378**

Lord, you have called your Church to shine as light
in the midst of a dark and needy world:
bless and strengthen it in its testimony in every land
for justice, truth, and freedom.
May it bring help and hope to the poor and the powerless,

to the outcast and the oppressed;
may it maintain a bold and fearless witness
in face of tyranny and wrong;
and may it never be ashamed of the gospel of Christ,
but point to him as the liberator of mankind,
the source of life and giver of peace.
We ask this in his name.

Your kingdom, O God, is among us **379**
as a seed growing secretly.
Let it burst into flower in our generation.
Where the poor are raised up,
there is your kingdom;
where justice flows down like the mountain streams,
there is your kingdom;
where men and women yield their lives to Christ and to the doing of his will,
there is the hidden treasure of your kingdom.
Help us, O God, to read the signs of the times,
to discern the kingdom's presence,
and to make it known in prophetic words
and committed lives;
through Jesus Christ our Lord. *John Kingsnorth*

380

Look in mercy, Lord, on the Church of your dear Son, here in our land and away to the ends of the earth.

Strengthen her witness for justice between man and man and between the nations, and her care and compassion for the weak and oppressed.

Call out from her men and women who will speak to the world, across all barriers of language and culture, of your mighty acts in Christ; to whom with you and the Spirit be all honour and glory, now and for ever. *John Kingsnorth*

THE CHURCH'S MISSION

The Church and the world **381**

O GOD, we are frightened by our world,
its cruelty and corruption, its greed and aggression,
and we look for a quiet corner where we can
live out our little lives in peace.
But we know in our hearts that this is cowardice.
Jesus our King has overcome all the dark forces of evil.
This sinful world is the world he has saved,
and we are called to make his salvation real
and to manifest it in our day.
Strengthen us, O Lord, for this task
by the indwelling of your Spirit,
and build up your Church everywhere in faith and love,
that the world may be released from its bondage
and enjoy the perfect freedom of your kingdom;
through Jesus Christ our Lord *John Kingsnorth*

382

Lord God, you have taught us to pray to you as "Our Father":
help us to see the world through your eyes
and to love your children with your love;
and show us how we can share with them
the knowledge of your Fatherhood
and an experience of your redeeming grace,
in your Son Jesus Christ our Lord.

Church Missionary Society

383

Heavenly Father, this world is very perplexing, and yet we believe in your love.

Our Church is far from perfect, yet we have met you in your family.

We feel so very small, and yet we know that your Son became a man to save us all.

Send your Spirit to help us to understand what you want us to do in the fellowship of your Church to bring the knowledge of your love to others in your world; through Jesus Christ our Lord. *Church Missionary Society*

The missionary Church **384**

Abba, Father, you have shown your great love
by sending Jesus into the world to give new life to men.
Pour your Spirit upon the Church
that it may preach the gospel to all in every place.
Call out men and women to reap the harvest-fields,
here in this country and beyond our shores.
May they see with the eyes of faith
the kingdom in our midst,
and reach forward in courage and hope
to the Kingdom that is to come. *John Kingsnorth*

385

O Saviour of the world,
lifted up on the cross to draw people
of all races and nations to yourself:
bless the witness of your Church
in this and every place,
and help us to finish the work
you have given us to do
in the world for which you died.

We ask it in your name,
our living and victorious Lord.

386

Heavenly Father, you have committed to your Church the good news of Jesus Christ to be shared with all mankind.

We confess with shame that we have been slow to fulfil this task and that multitudes have never yet heard of Jesus.

Forgive our failure, our disobedience, our lack of love;
rekindle our zeal, enlarge our vision, increase our faith;
and show us each one what you would have us to do in the service of your world-wide kingdom; through Jesus Christ our Lord. *Frank Colquhoun*

See also 51–2

Today's missionaries **387**

Eternal Father, it is your joy to call men and women to serve you across the barriers of race and language and culture: give them strength and courage in your service, and satisfy their longing to make known the good news of Jesus Christ.

When they are in danger, save them from fear.
When they are disheartened, be their friend.
When they think they have failed, show them the cross.

Give them peace in their hearts, and peace in their homes, and the joy of acceptance by those whom they serve; for Jesus Christ's sake. *John Kingsnorth*

Our part in mission **388**

Heavenly Father, you have called your Church
to proclaim the gospel in all lands,
and to gather the people of all races
into the fellowship of Christ's Church.

Help us in obedience to your call
to participate actively in the Christian mission,
in our own country and overseas,
and to commend the gospel of Christ
by what we are,
by what we say,
and by what we do for others,
to the glory of your name.

Derived from the CMS Basis of Membership

389

Teach us, O God, that as members of your worldwide Church we are all involved in its mission to share the good news of Jesus Christ with mankind.

Show us what this means for each of us personally:
in equipping ourselves for your service;
in bearing witness to the gospel where we live and work;
in serving the Church here at home;
and in supporting its work overseas by our prayers and gifts.

May all we do, O Lord, be a grateful response to your immeasurable love in the redemption of the world by our Lord Jesus Christ; to whom be glory now and for ever.

Frank Colquhoun

The unconverted **390**

God and Father of us all, you loved the world so much
that you gave your only Son for the salvation of mankind.
We pray for those who are strangers to your love:
for those in spiritual darkness
who have not heard the gospel of Christ,
and for those who having heard it
have chosen darkness rather than light.
In your great mercy draw them to yourself

through him who was lifted up on the cross,
that they may receive the gift of eternal life in him,
our Lord and Saviour Jesus Christ.

Llewellyn Cumings
Based on John 3. 14–18

391

Merciful Father, lover of souls and redeemer of mankind, have compassion on all who do not know you as you are revealed in your Son Jesus Christ.

Let your gospel be preached with grace and power to those who have not known it; turn the hearts of those who resist it; and bring home to your fold those who have gone astray; that there may be one flock under one shepherd, Jesus Christ our Lord. *Episcopal Church, U.S.A.*

Those of other religions **392**

Heavenly Father, help us to be willing to learn more about the world's religions, so that we may understand our differences and share common convictions, and go forward in faith to grasp more of the truth you have revealed to us in your Son, Jesus Christ our Lord.

*Bible Reading Fellowship**

393

Eternal God, you have shown yourself to mankind in many forms:
each has glimpsed one colour of your rainbow truth.
Help us to share that truth with one another,
until in the fullness of time the glory is revealed
and we see clearly the one Lord to whom all worship is offered.
But keep us as Christians faithful to the light
you have given us, shining in the face of Jesus

You may lead other men and other worlds in other ways, but for us he is your Word: the Way, the Truth, and the Life.

Stanley Pritchard

Communicating the gospel **394**

We thank you, our Father, for the revelation of your will and love in Jesus Christ, who is your living Word and express Image.

Inspire with wisdom, insight and imagination those who seek by every technique of sight and sound to communicate the truth of the gospel to others, that they may know your love and learn your will shown to us by word and image in Jesus Christ our Lord. *Basil Naylor*

395

O Holy Spirit of God, who on the day of Pentecost unified the language of men, so that your messengers were able to speak the gospel to people of many nations: grant to your Church in our generation so to enter into the experience and thinking of men and women, that its message may go home to their hearts and make known the saving love of him who from his cross is ever drawing all men to himself, even Jesus Christ, the Lord of all and the Saviour of all.

*Feed the Minds**

396

Father, as we seek to share the gospel with others, help us to present it as the good news it really is: the good news of your amazing love and liberating power made known in Jesus Christ.

Help us to share it with conviction, as those who believe its truth;

with urgency, as those who know the task is pressing and the time is short;

and above all with gratitude, as those who have found in Jesus a living Saviour and Lord. We ask it in his name.

Frank Colquhoun

Missionary societies **397**

We give you thanks, our Father, for the missionary societies of the Church and for those who have gone forth within their fellowship to preach the gospel and further your kingdom in every part of the world.

We thank you for all who in years past have supported and maintained this work; and we pray that we in our own day may not fail to do our part, and so share in the Church's mission to make disciples of all the nations, for the sake of Jesus Christ our Lord. *Frank Colquhoun*

Bible societies **398**

Father, help us who love and treasure the holy scriptures to be faithful in sending your written word to places where we cannot go and in making it available to people whose language we cannot speak.

We thank you that this is possible through the work of the Bible societies throughout the world.

Prosper and multiply their endeavours, that increasing multitudes may read the scriptures in their mother tongue and learn of your saving love, revealed to us in your Son, Jesus Christ our Lord. *Adapted*

Christian literature **399**

Almighty God, you hallowed words to be an instrument of your Word: we ask you to direct and prosper the work of Christian writers and translators, and of all who distribute Christian literature, and to use their endeavours to the advancement of true knowledge, righteousness and holiness among the nations of the world; through Jesus Christ our Lord. *Feed the Minds**

The Anglican Communion: partners in mission **400**

Almighty God, you have called the churches of the Anglican Communion to witness and service, and have richly blessed them.

Grant that the members of this world-wide family may plan and work together in brotherly love to further your mission to the world. And confessing that the Church which lives to itself will die by itself, may we receive humbly, give generously, and share joyfully the spiritual treasures and material resources you have entrusted to us; through our Lord and Saviour Jesus Christ. *John Kingsnorth*

THE CHURCH'S MINISTRY

The ministry of the whole Church **401**

We thank you, our Father, that you call us all to your service as members of the Body of Christ. Every one of us has a vocation to fulfil, a ministry to exercise.

We thank you that your whole Church is a holy priesthood, and that it is the privilege of each of us to offer spiritual sacrifices, to enter into the Holiest, to intercede for the world, to introduce others to Jesus.

Help us to see this more clearly, and show us what it means for our own life and service, for the glory of Christ our Lord. *Frank Colquhoun*

402

Father, may your Holy Spirit kindle in all our hearts
a greater love for Christ and his Church,
and make us fully alive to the opportunities of service
which are ours in today's world.
Save us from complacency and fear of new ways;
inspire us with the vision of a world won for you;
and stir our wills to pray and work and give
until your will is done on earth as in heaven;
through Jesus Christ our Lord.

Commitment to service **403**

Lord, we have but one life to live,
the life you have given us,
the life you have redeemed.
Help us to make the best use of it

and not to waste it or fritter it away.
Show us your plan and purpose for our life,
and let it be our joy to do your will
and serve you all our days.
Lord, let us not live to be useless,
for Jesus Christ's sake. *Frank Colquhoun*

404

Lord God, whose we are and whom we serve:
we place our lives afresh in your hands.
Take us as we are,
and make us what you would have us to be;
and so fill us with your Holy Spirit
that we may be strong for your service
and used wholly for your glory;
through Jesus Christ our Lord. *Frank Colquhoun*

Differing gifts **405**

Lord of the Church,
you have given your servants differing gifts,
that they may share them with others
in the household of faith
and use them responsibly
in the service of the world:
grant us to be generous in giving
and humble in receiving,
that we may grow up to mature manhood
and attain to the full stature of Christ.
John Kingsnorth

Priorities **406**

Lord God, may we never forget that the Church exists in the world not for its own sake but for your glory and the service of mankind.

Save us as church people from getting wrapped up in our own affairs and the mundane things that absorb so much of our time and money and energy.

Help us to get our priorities right: to seek first your kingdom and the hallowing of your name;

to obey our Lord's command to preach the gospel everywhere and to everyone;

to minister for his sake to the poor, the afflicted, and the oppressed;

and to practice the royal law by loving our neighbour as ourselves.

Give us a new vision of what the Church should be, and of your purpose for it, here and in every place; through Jesus Christ our Lord. *Frank Colquhoun*

Christ's witnesses **407**

Lord, you have called us to be your witnesses in the world: give us grace to hear and obey your call.

Release us from the bondage of anxiety and fear; restore us to love, joy and peace as we trust in you; and so strengthen us by your Holy Spirit that by word and good example we may glorify you in our daily lives; through Jesus Christ our Lord.

*Church Missionary Society**

408

We thank you, Lord, for calling us to be your witnesses: grant us the courage and the love to be obedient and faithful to that calling.

We pray that our lives may bear witness to your love shown in Jesus Christ, and that our witness may reflect your light in the communities in which we live and work, to the glory of your name. *Basil Naylor*

The servant Church **409**

Lord Christ, you came among us
as the Servant of the Lord.
Your whole life here on earth was dedicated
to the doing of the Father's will
and to ministering to those in need;
and at the last you crowned your service with your sacrifice,
and gave your life for the salvation of mankind.
May the Church which professes your name follow this pattern,
and be seen everywhere as a serving community,
giving itself for the sake of others;
and may your law of love and sacrifice
be written in all our lives,
that we may rightly call you Lord. *Frank Colquhoun*

Ministers of the Church **410**

We thank you, O God, for those whom you have called through the centuries to serve in the ministry of the Church.

Pour your blessing on those whom you have called today [and especially on your servant(s) whom we now remember]; that by word and deed they may bear witness to your saving love and power, and enable your people to grow up into him who is the Head, our Lord and Saviour Jesus Christ, to whom be praise and honour for ever. *Adapted*

411

Lord God, we pray for your Church's ministers.
May they have strength for their work,
and grow in holiness and love.
May they be mature in their faith
and wise in their judgments.
May they be confident of your grace

and zealous in fulfilling their duties.
May they boldly proclaim the truth of your Word
and faithfully administer your sacraments.
And may they seek your glory in all things,
through Jesus Christ our Lord. *ACCM**

412

Lord Jesus Christ,
Apostle, Priest and Servant,
bless those whom you have called to the ministry
as bishops, priests, and deacons.
May they lead your people courageously,
care for them lovingly, teach them faithfully,
and send them forth to be your witnesses in the world;
for your name's sake. *ACCM**

413

Lord Jesus, the great Shepherd of the sheep,
we pray for your under-shepherds who care for your flock
as ministers of the gospel.
Keep them faithful when things are difficult
and humble when things go well.
May your word be in their hearts and on their lips,
and may they commend you to others
by what they are as well as by what they say;
for the glory of your name.

Teachers of the Faith **414**

Lord Jesus Christ, who patiently taught your disciples, and whom the people gladly heard: may your words so master our hearts and minds that we too may teach with skill and authority, and be heard with joy and understanding; for your name's sake. *Timothy Dudley-Smith*

The wholeness of the Church's ministry **415**

Almighty God, you have committed to men and women the ministry of the gospel.

Pour your grace on all whom you call to this ministry in our day; and give to your Church wisdom in the ordering of their vocations, that together they may forward your purposes of love to all people; through Jesus Christ our Lord.

John Poulton

CHURCH UNITY

Unity in Christ **416**

GOD our Father, in whose will is our peace, forgive us for our differences and divisions which keep us apart from one another; and enable the separated branches of your Church to find their essential unity in Christ, our one Lord; that in fellowship with him we may preserve the unity which the Spirit gives, and demonstrate to the world the reconciling power of the gospel, to the glory of your name.

Frank Colquhoun

417

Lord and heavenly Father,
through your Son Jesus Christ
you have called us to be one
  in the family of your Church:
give us grace to break down the barriers
  which keep us apart;
that, accepting our differences,
we may grow in love for one another,
  to the glory of your name;
through Jesus Christ our Lord.

418

Lord Christ, by whose cross all enmity is ended
  and all walls of separation broken down:
look with compassion on the anguish of your world
  and the broken body of your Church;
and by the power of the Holy Spirit
  heal our divisions,
  unite us in your truth,
and make us instruments of your peace
  in the life of the world,
to the glory of God the Father. *Adapted*

Penitence **419**

O God, the one Father of each and of all, forgive our too narrow claims to be loyal.

Forgive our efforts to structure the Spirit, and our hardness of hearing when you speak with the accents of other perceptions and of other traditions.

Break us, remake us one holy people, one with the oneness you have in living, in loving, in giving in Trinity.

John Kingsnorth

420

Son of God, our Saviour, who prayed that we all might be one: we confess before you our failure to maintain the unity of the Spirit, and our indifference to the scandal of a divided Church in a divided world.

Have mercy upon us, O Lord, and forgive us.

Disturb our complacency; deepen our concern; arouse us to fresh endeavours, and strengthen the bonds of peace; that your Church may be seen to be one Body, acknowledging one Lord, proclaiming one faith, and worshipping one God and Father; to whom be glory for ever. *Frank Colquhoun*

The healing of divisions **421**

Holy and undivided Trinity, Father, Son, and Holy Spirit, heal our divisions and make us one, as you are one.

God the Father, draw us nearer to one another in your family of the Church.

God the Son, reconcile our differences and break down our barriers by the power of your cross;

God the Holy Spirit, deepen our fellowship and strengthen the bonds of peace.

So may we, as one people, with one heart and mind, glorify you, the one eternal God, now and for ever.

Frank Colquhoun

Brotherly love **422**

We praise you, O God, for the fellowship of the Spirit
who unites us in the bond of peace
as members of the one Body.
Deepen our communion with one another in Christ,
and grant that through your Spirit continually working in us
we may daily increase in the knowledge of your love,
and learn to love our brethren with the love
you have shown us in your Son,
our Lord and Saviour Jesus Christ. *Basil Naylor*

Unity and mission **423**

God and Father of us all, we give thanks for the spiritual unity which is already ours as believers in the one Lord and members of the one Body.

We pray that this spiritual unity may, by your grace, increasingly become a visible unity, so that your Church in every place may demonstrate the healing and reconciling power of the gospel and be an instrument of your peace in the life of the world, to the praise and glory of your name.

Frank Colquhoun

424

Heavenly Father, whose will it is
that your Church should be one visible body,
so that the world might see and believe:
draw us and all your people closer to him
who is the one Head, Jesus Christ,
so that we may come closer to one another;
and unite us all in a common concern
to share your good news with others
and further your kingdom here on earth,
in the name of Christ our Lord.

Frank Colquhoun

Those from whom we differ **425**

Lord, your love knows no bounds,
no limits, no distinctions.
We pray for those from whom we differ
in religion, in race, in politics.
Help us to respect their point of view
and to love them as they are loved by you,
recognizing that as everywhere is your country,
so every man is our neighbour.

Racial harmony in the Church **426**

God and Father of us all, through the death and resurrection of your Son Jesus Christ you have overcome the sin which separates us from you and from one another: so shed your love abroad in our hearts by the Holy Spirit that in the fellowship of the Church we may disregard every consideration of race and colour, and see in all fellow Christians our brothers and sisters for whom the Saviour died, and love them as he loves us; for his name's sake.

Adapted

An act of commitment **427**

God our Father, it is your purpose
to bring the whole creation into full unity in Christ.
We commit ourselves to you, that by your grace
we may further this your will on earth.
Help us to live for others even as your love includes all;
to seek out from others the truth they have grasped;
to trust each other as our fellow workers
in the one community you have given us;
and to obey your call to make visible the unity of your Church.
Come, Holy Spirit, and help us,
through Christ our Lord.

*Prayer for Christian Unity 1978**

IX
THE CHURCH IN THE PARISH

THE PARISH

Parish and people **428**

GOD our Father, graciously hallow with your blessing
this our parish church.
May it be a place where the sorrowing find comfort
and the tempted strength;
where the lonely find fellowship
and the sinner forgiveness;
where the faithful find grace,
and all offer you a holy worship;
in the name of Jesus Christ our Lord. *Adapted*

429

Almighty God, we pray for your blessing on all who share in the life and work of this church:
in the ministry of word and sacrament,
in teaching and pastoral care,
in service to the diocese, the community, and those in need,
in ecumenical fellowship and co-operation.

We pray for all members of the congregation, that in their varied callings they may advance your kingdom and bear witness to your love, shown in your Son Jesus Christ our Lord. *Basil Naylor*

430

Bless, O Lord our God,
the worship and work of this church,
that it may be a house of prayer,

a centre of Christian teaching,
a community of service,
and a witness to your redeeming love;
through Jesus Christ our Lord.

431

Save us, O Lord, as a parish, from being inward-looking or backward-looking in the work of this church.

Help us to take our eyes off ourselves and turn them on the world around; to be concerned less with what we have accomplished and more with what remains to be done; that with our vision enlarged and our love rekindled we may go forward to attempt new and greater things to your glory, in the name of Jesus Christ our Lord. *Frank Colquhoun*

432

Lord Jesus Christ,
as you have called the Church out of the world
to bring the world to yourself,
so we pray for your Church in this parish;
that all may worship you with singleness of mind,
that all may hold the faith in sincerity and love,
and all may witness for you with courage and assurance,
for the glory of your name.

*Church Pastoral Aid Society**

Patronal festival **433**

Almighty God, to whose glory we celebrate the dedication of this house of prayer: we give you thanks for the fellowship of those who have worshipped in this place; and we pray that all who seek you here may find you, and be filled with your joy and peace; through Jesus Christ our Lord.

Episcopal Church, U.S.A.

434

Almighty God, to whom is due all praise and honour, look graciously upon us who give thanks for the foundation of this church and its life down the years.

As you have put your name in this place, bless its witness to our day, and for generations yet to come.

Inspire us with your Spirit; move our hearts to give and to work in your service; accept our worship, and build us up a spiritual temple, a holy priesthood, to offer sacrifices acceptable to you, through Jesus Christ our Lord.

John Poulton

See also 60

Stewardship **435**

We praise you, our Father, for the abundant and inexhaustible riches which you lavish upon us in Christ as members of your Church.

Help us to respond to your love in terms of our wealth and possessions, and to act always as responsible stewards of your grace; that we may give as freely as we have received, and do all in the name of him who gave his all for us, Jesus our Saviour and our Lord.

436

Almighty God, you have made us members of Christ and of his Church, and have taught us through him that it is more blessed to give than to receive: make us truly thankful for all your goodness; help us to deepen our commitment to you as stewards of our time, talents, and money; and guide us in all things to know and do your will, for the honour and glory of your name.

A parish mission **437**

Heavenly Father, we thank you for your love for us
revealed in your Son Jesus Christ.
You call us to make your love known to others
in this parish and neighbourhood.
Help each one of us to respond to this challenge
as we prepare for the forthcoming mission;
and grant that in the coming days
many may come to a knowledge of your love
and give their lives to your service;
for Jesus Christ's sake. *Frank Colquhoun*

New converts **438**

Most gracious God, we thank you for those among us who have newly entered into the joy of your salvation and dedicated their lives to your service.

May they never cease to wonder at what, by your grace, you have done for them.

Help them to continue firmly in the faith of Christ, to bear witness to your love, and to let the Holy Spirit mould their characters; and grant that all their future days may be lived to your greater glory; for Jesus' sake.

Evangelistic visiting **439**

We remember, O Lord, that the apostle Paul proclaimed the gospel not only in public places but also from house to house.

Give grace to us your servants as we seek to spread the good news of Jesus by visiting the homes of this parish.

Keep us humble and make us wise;
show us how to use our opportunities;
help us to speak a word in season;

and in all we say and do may we commend our Master and further his kingdom, to the glory of your name.

Michael Botting

Parish publicity **440**

Heavenly Father, assist us in our efforts to make contact with the homes and people of our parish by means of the magazine, posters, leaflets, and other literature.

Grant that our publicity may not be misleading, or unworthy, or trite, but may truly represent us as your people, and commend him who is our good news, Jesus Christ our Lord.

Christopher Idle

A vestry prayer before worship **441**

LORD and heavenly Father,
make us mindful of your presence with us
in this hour of worship;
that we may draw near to you
with holy and humble hearts,
and offer prayers and praises
acceptable in your sight;
through Jesus Christ our Lord.

Frank Colquhoun

Preparation for Holy Communion **442**

Lord Jesus Christ, we thank you for giving us the sacrament of Holy Communion, to be to us and your whole Church

a memorial of your passion,
a pledge of your redeeming love,
a means of spiritual grace,
and a foretaste of the heavenly banquet.

Make these things real to us, O Christ, when we partake of the sacrament.

Above all, make yourself real to us as our living Saviour and Lord, ever to be honoured, worshipped and adored.

Frank Colquhoun

443

O Lamb of God,
Saviour of the world,
be to us at every eucharist
the heavenly Bread,
the true Vine;
that we may feed on your body and blood
by faith,
lift up our hearts
with thanksgiving,
and present ourselves to you
a living sacrifice,
to your glory. *Frank Colquhoun*

444

Lord Jesus, help us to draw near to your table
with obedient hearts,
in response to your own invitation;
with penitent hearts,
acknowledging our need of forgiveness;
with expectant hearts,
knowing that you are present to meet with us;
with grateful hearts,
as those for whom your body was broken,
your blood shed.
Make us ready to receive all that you have for us,
and to give all of ourselves to you;
for your great love's sake. *Frank Colquhoun*

The housebound **445**

Lord Jesus Christ, the friend of the helpless and companion of the lonely, we ask your blessing on those who are unable to leave their homes and join in public worship.

Give them the assurance of your presence with them, and of their oneness with the whole family of your Church; that in heart and mind they may worship you, O Christ, who with the Father and the Holy Spirit lives and reigns one God for evermore. *Andrew Warner*

The crèche **446**

We thank you, Lord Jesus, that you showed your love for little children when you blessed those brought to you by their parents.

We ask your blessing on the children in our crèche today during this hour of worship.

May the Christian love of the helpers show these little ones something of your love, and contribute to their spiritual upbringing in the family of the Church; for your name's sake. *Michael Botting*

Offertory prayers **447**

Heavenly Father, may these gifts go where we cannot go,
and help those whom we cannot reach.
Through them may the ignorant be taught,
the hungry fed, the sick healed,
and the lost found, for Jesus' sake. *Stanley Pritchard*

448

Lord, not our gifts alone
but our lives also we now offer to you.
Accept both them and us
  in your service,
and use both them and us
  for your glory,
through Christ our Lord. *Frank Colquhoun*

Church musicians and artists **449**

O God, whom saints and angels delight to worship in heaven: be ever present with your servants who seek through art and music to perfect the praises offered by your people on earth.

Grant to them even now glimpses of your beauty; and make us all more worthy at length to behold it unveiled for evermore; through Jesus Christ our Lord.

Episcopal Church, U.S.A.

For a church porch **450**

Be silent, be thoughtful, be reverent,
  for this is the house of the Lord.
Before the service, speak to God.
During the service, let God speak to you.
After the service, speak to one another.

Charmaine Host

Parochial church council

451

MOST merciful Father, as we meet together in your service we commit ourselves to you for the tasks that lie before us and the decisions we shall be called upon to make.

So guide us with your fatherly wisdom, and cleanse our hearts from all self-seeking, that we may resolve only those things that will promote your glory and further the work you have entrusted to us in this parish; through Jesus Christ our Lord. *Adapted*

452

Father, we seek the guidance of your Holy Spirit
in all the business that lies before us.
In planning for the future, give us vision;
in matters of finance, give us responsibility;
in dealing with people, give us love.
Help us in all things to honour your name,
to advance your kingdom,
and to carry out your will;
through Jesus Christ our Lord. *Adapted*

A church meeting

453

God our Father, as we meet in the name of your Son Jesus Christ make us to know your presence with us, and in all our thinking and speaking keep us in harmony with your will.

Give us a vision of your kingdom, insight into your purposes, and understanding of the needs of your work.

We place ourselves at your disposal. We are your fellow workers, eager and ready to carry out your wishes.

Use us, O Lord, as you will, and for your glory.

A church conference **454**

God of all grace, wisdom and power, we lift up our hearts to you in prayer as we take counsel together at this time in the service of your Church.

Make us sensitive and responsive to the guidance of your Holy Spirit;

bring all our plans and decisions into conformity with your perfect will;

and use all our endeavours for the furtherance of the gospel, the good of your people, and the glory of our Lord and Saviour Jesus Christ.

A quiet day or retreat **455**

Father, as we meet together in this place, help us to listen, to understand, and to remember.

Make us aware that we are meeting not simply with one another but with you. Let your presence be real to each one of us.

As we pray, may it be just like speaking with you.

As we listen, help us to concentrate, so that we really hear your word, and take in and retain what is said.

And when we finish, enable us by your grace to go out and put into practice all that you tell us to do; and to your name be glory, through Jesus Christ our Lord.

Confirmation candidates **456**

God of all grace and power, we ask your blessing on those who are receiving instruction and preparing for confirmation.

May your Holy Spirit so work in their hearts and minds that they may fully commit themselves to Jesus Christ and acknowledge him as Lord; and grant that they may continue steadfast in the faith and fellowship of the Church until their lives end. *Frank Colquhoun*

After confirmation **457**

Heavenly Father, you have given your servants grace boldly to confess their faith and to dedicate themselves to your service.

Help them to put Christ first in every part of their lives, and by the diligent use of the means of grace to grow in the knowledge of his love.

Strengthen them daily by your Holy Spirit, and keep them faithful members of your Church all the days of their life; for the sake of Jesus Christ our Lord. *Martin Parsons*

Young people **458**

God our Father, we pray for our young people growing up in an unstable and confusing world.

Show them that your ways give more meaning to life than the ways of the world, and that following you is better than chasing after selfish goals.

Help them to take failure not as a measure of their worth, but as a chance for a new start.

Give them strength to hold their faith in you, and to keep alive their joy in your creation; through Jesus Christ our Lord. *Episcopal Church, U.S.A.*

459

We pray, our Father, for the teenagers of our church.

Help us who are older to remember the adventure and joy of youth as well as the temptations and frustrations; and enable us to assist our young people by our prayers, our example, and our friendship.

Help those in their teens to respond to the love of Jesus, to yield him their allegiance, and to serve him as Lord and Saviour all their days; for his name's sake.

Michael Botting

Those preparing for examinations **460**

God, all-wise, all-loving, we pray for those among us who are preparing for examinations.

Give them diligence to persevere in their studies, and clarity of mind to grasp and retain what they learn.

Help them to acquit themselves worthily in their exams, to give of their best and to leave the issue in your hands.

We ask it in Christ's name.

Youth: a prayer of dedication **461**

Lord Jesus, in the morning of our lives,
while we are young and fit and strong,
we want to give ourselves to you.
Take all our powers of mind and body
and harness them to your service.
May we not squander our days
on the passing things of the world,
but dedicate them to the service of your kingdom
and the doing of your will;
that till life shall end
we may be your faithful servants
and seek in all things to glorify you,
our Saviour and our King.

Frank Colquhoun

Bible study group **462**

Heavenly Father, we thank you for the Bible and all that it has meant to your Church through the centuries in the building up of its faith and life.

Assist us now in our study of it.

May the Spirit of truth guide us into all truth, and lead us to him who is the Truth incarnate, Jesus Christ our Lord.

Frank Colquhoun

463

God our Father, we have met together
in the name of our Lord Jesus Christ
to study the scriptures and learn more of your truth.
Open our minds to the light of your word
and grant us the guidance of your Holy Spirit;
that as we think and talk together
we may discover your will and purpose for our lives,
and be better equipped to serve you in the world,
to the honour and glory of your name.

Llewellyn Cumings

Young mothers' group **464**

We praise you, Lord Jesus, that through your holy birth at Bethlehem you raised the status of motherhood.

We bring before you everything that being a mother means to us.

We offer you all our joys and frustrations, our ambitions and disappointments, our hopes and our fears.

Thank you that you understand and care about them all.

Michael Botting

465

Heavenly Father, we ask your blessing on our mothers' fellowship:

that as we share our problems and encourage one another we may grow in Christian love and understanding;

that as we learn more of your truth and of yourself we may have a stronger faith;

and that as we serve you in our daily lives your Holy Spirit may bring forth fruit in us that will reflect Christ to our families and to all around; for his name's sake.

Michael Botting

Community action groups **466**

We thank you, O God, for our local community groups and for the opportunities of joint action they give us.

When we cannot fight alone for truth and justice,
help us to draw strength from one another.
When we cannot unite on every detail of policy or belief,
help us to work together for limited objectives.
When we cannot agree with our neighbours,
help us still to love them.

Draw us together in a fellowship of service, and embody in us the good news of your kingdom; through Jesus Christ our Lord.

Christopher Idle

Prayer for use by a team of workers **467**

Grant us, Lord, as your fellow workers,
humility and self-effacement in our service together,
the art of listening to one another,
the readiness to accept the team's decisions,
an understanding of our different characters,
and the ability to maintain creative relationships.
We ask it in the name of our one Master, Jesus Christ.

Basil Naylor

Funerals **468**

O GOD, whose days are without end, and whose mercies cannot be numbered: make us, we pray, deeply aware of the shortness and uncertainty of human life; and let your Holy Spirit lead us in holiness and righteousness all our days; that, when we have served you in our generation, we may be gathered to our ancestors, having the testimony of a good conscience, in the communion of the Catholic Church, in the confidence of a certain faith, in favour with you, our God, and in perfect charity with the world. All this we ask through Jesus Christ our Lord.

Episcopal Church, U.S.A.

469

God of grace and glory, we remember before you this day our *brother N.*

We thank you for giving *him* to us, his family and friends, to know and to love as a companion on our earthly pilgrimage.

In your boundless compassion console us who mourn; and give us faith to see in death the gate of eternal life, so that in quiet confidence we may continue our course on earth, until, by your call, we are reunited with those who have gone before; through Jesus Christ our Lord.

Episcopal Church, U.S.A.

470

Almighty God, we rejoice to know
that your reign extends far beyond
the limits of this life.
In the mystery of what lies beyond our sight
we pray that your love may complete its work
in those whose days on earth are done;
and grant that we who serve you now in this world
may at last share with them
the glories of your heavenly kingdom;
through the love of Jesus Christ our Lord.

471

Welcome, O Lord, into the joy and peace of your kingdom those who have departed out of this life to be with you.

Mercifully grant them a place with the spirits of the just; and give them the life that knows not age, the reward that passes not away; through the merits of our Lord and Saviour Jesus Christ. *Adapted from St. Ignatius Loyola*

See also 316–21

Memorial services

472

God our Father, we praise your holy name
for all who have lived and died in the faith of Christ
and are now at rest in him.
Especially at this time we remember your servants . . .
Their example has encouraged us,
their witness has inspired us,
and the memory of them makes us glad today.
For them all we thank you,
we honour and we worship you,
as they do now by your grace and in your glory;
through Jesus Christ our Lord. *Christopher Idle*

473

God of the living and Father of our risen Lord,
we are glad in your presence today
as we remember those who have gone before us
  believing your promises
  and trusting in your mercy.
Help us to follow them,
  as they followed Christ,
and with all your people on earth and in heaven
to give you the glory and the praise
  that is your due;
through Jesus Christ our Lord. *Christopher Idle*

474

Lord, teach us so to number our days
  that we may apply our hearts to wisdom.
Help us by your grace to use aright
the time that is left to us here on earth:
  to remember the needs of others,
  to serve and help those in trouble,
and so to live that we may not be afraid to die;
  through Jesus Christ our Lord.

Frank Colquhoun

475

We give them back to you, dear Lord, who gave them to us. Yet as you do not lose them in giving, so we have not lost them by their return.

Not as the world gives do you give, O Lover of souls. What you gave you do not take away; for what is ours is ours always, if we are yours. And life is eternal, and love is immortal, and death is only an horizon, and an horizon is nothing save the limit of our sight.

Lift us, strong Son of God, that we may see farther.

Cleanse our eyes that we may see more clearly.

Draw us closer to yourself that we may know ourselves nearer to them. And while you are preparing a place for us, prepare us for that happy place, that where they are and you are, we too may be; through Jesus Christ our Lord.

476

Receive, Lord, into the arms of your everlasting mercy your servant *N.*, whom we lovingly and gratefully remember before you this day.

May the good work which you began in *him* here be brought to completion on the day of Christ; that as *he* hoped and trusted in you in this life, so you will be *his* strength, *his* song, and *his* exceeding great reward in the life to come; through Jesus Christ, our Saviour and Redeemer.

VARIOUS

The diocese **477**

O GOD, by your grace you have called us in this diocese to a goodly fellowship of faith: bless our Bishop(s) *N.* [and *N.*], and other clergy, and all your people.

Grant that your word may be truly preached and truly heard, your sacraments be faithfully administered and faithfully received.

By your Spirit fashion our lives according to the example of your Son, and grant that we may show the power of your love to all among whom we live; through Jesus Christ our Lord. *Episcopal Church, U.S.A.*

Before a concert or choral festival **478**

Lord God, the eternal spring of all that is worthy and lovely in our world, we thank you for the gift of music.

Let the mystery and power of its inspiration draw us into closer fellowship with you and into deeper gratitude for all your blessings upon us, now and always; through Jesus Christ our Lord. *Alan Warren*

Grace at a parish lunch **479**

Lord Jesus, we remember how you brought blessing
to many meal times when on earth:
sharing a wedding feast,
feeding the five thousand,
having breakfast by the seaside.
Bless our food and fellowship today.

May this be a time when we experience your risen presence,
and get to know some people better,
and others for the first time;
for your name's sake. *Michael Botting*

Counselling **480**

We bring to you, our God, in the name of the Lord Jesus Christ, those whom we shall seek to help this *week* through the ministry of counselling.

Teach us afresh the disciplines of silence and speech, of patience and directness; that every personal encounter may be an experience of your presence and an unfolding of your grace; for Jesus Christ's sake. *Christopher Idle*

Interviews **481**

Heavenly Father, the only wise God,
help those who are to be interviewed this day [*or* week]
to be clear in their thinking,
truthful in their speaking,
and above all to be themselves.
And help the interviewers
to ask questions that are fair,
to discover facts that are relevant,
and to make decisions that are right.
Grant this for Christ our Saviour's sake.

Christopher Idle

Vergers **482**

You have taught us, O God, that every member of Christ's Body has a ministry to exercise for the good of the whole community: hear us as we pray for those who exercise their ministry as vergers in our churches.

Give them health of body, discernment of spirit, and skill of hand; that with courtesy, tact and patience they may fulfil their calling, and meet the varied demands made upon them in the ordering of the worship and service of your house, to the glory of your name. *Basil Naylor*

Victims of the cults **483**

God of all grace, enlighten the minds and turn the hearts of those who have been corrupted or misled by the false teaching of the cults.

May your Holy Spirit show them their errors and lead them to the truth as it is in Jesus, the only Saviour and the one Lord; for your tender mercy's sake.

Christopher Idle

484

O God of truth, bring into the way of truth, we pray, all whose minds are at variance with your truth; through him who is the Way and the Truth, your Son Jesus Christ our Lord. *Henry Cooper*

Holidays **485**

Heavenly Father, we thank you for the times of rest and relaxation which are given to us in the course of our lives.

Teach us to use our leisure and our holidays to rebuild our bodies and renew our minds; and may we be strengthened and refreshed in spirit for our daily work and the service of your kingdom; through Jesus Christ our Lord.

Episcopal Church, U.S.A.

Before a bank holiday **486**

O God, the giver of all good things,
we pray for those who use the roads today
and for all who travel at this holiday time;
that they may set out in peace
  and return in safety,

refreshed in body, mind and spirit;
and that seeing the glory of your works
they may remember to give you
  their thanks and praise
for Jesus Christ's sake. *Christopher Idle*

Village churches **487**

Lord Jesus Christ, you entered many villages of Palestine and so brought the kingdom of God near to the people living in them.

We pray for the spiritual needs of the villages in our land today, especially those where church services are infrequent or where church buildings have been closed.

Raise up in such places dedicated Christians who are prepared to serve you in the community and exercise pastoral care and oversight; that in every village there may be a witness to you and the gospel, for the glory of your name.

Llewellyn Cumings

X
PASTORAL PRAYERS

Note on Pastoral Prayers

The prayers in this section are intended for use not in public worship but in specific pastoral situations. They are of a varied character and fall, generally speaking, into two classes.

Some of the prayers (the majority in fact) are designed to be said by the pastor or counsellor dealing with the situation; others are for use by the person or persons in need of pastoral help.

In the former case, the prayers should be regarded primarily as a guide to the sort of prayers that may prove useful on such occasions rather than as actual forms of prayer to be strictly adhered to in their printed form. In many instances they will have to be adapted to meet the particular needs and circumstances of those involved.

In the other case, it is suggested that the prayer in question (suitably altered if necessary) should be written out and given to the persons concerned for their private use. It is a fact that many people in times of trouble or distress sincerely desire to pray but find it difficult to put their thoughts into words. In such cases a short and simple form of prayer may meet their need and help them to lift up their hearts to God.

F.C.

MARRIAGE AND FAMILY LIFE

God's will concerning marriage **488**

HEAVENLY Father, we know that marriage is of your ordaining, and that your Son blessed by his presence the wedding at Cana in Galilee.

But we also learn from his example and teaching that marriage is not your will for everyone.

Grant to each of us personally the knowledge of your will, the grace to accept it, and the power of your Spirit to obey it; for in your will alone we find true peace and fulfilment, and your ultimate glory. *Michael Botting*

Those about to be married **489**

Lord, bless those who are soon to be married, especially these your servants *N.* and *N.*

In the rush of all the preparations grant them a deepening conviction of their love for each other and the knowledge that this love is your gift to them.

Help them so completely to trust one another that they may be able to face the unknown future with confidence and hope; through Jesus Christ our Lord.

*Mothers' Union Service Book**

490

Our loving heavenly Father, we commit to you these your servants who come to you seeking your blessing upon their marriage.

Keep them close to you and to one another; and may your grace so rest upon them that they may be faithful to the promises and vows that they will make, and may know your peace and presence throughout their wedded life; for the sake of Jesus Christ our Lord. *Frank Colquhoun*

491

God our Father, we remember young people planning their lives together and preparing for the commitment of marriage.

May they face their future with realism, recognizing that the sun does not always shine, that pain sometimes enters happiness, and that each is an individual with a viewpoint and a need.

May they maintain their personal independence, their sense of humour, their understanding of human frailty, and their capacity for forgiveness and trust.

Neither in prosperity nor in adversity may they grow apart or become unmindful of the vows they once made; and at all times may they be strengthened by the sure grasp of their love for one another, and your love for them.

Stanley Pritchard

Thanksgiving for the birth of a child **492**

We rejoice before you, Creator God, in all your marvellous works.

We bless you for the miracle of new life, and that you have called men and women to share in this wonder.

Today we especially thank you for the safe delivery of this child; praying that *he* may grow physically to healthy adulthood, and spiritually to know and love you, whom to know is eternal life, in Jesus Christ our Lord.

Michael Botting

493

Father, we remember before you those who have known the joy of a birth in their home.

We are grateful for a life given, and for a life spared.

As we share the gladness of the parents, we pray that you will grant them the wisdom, the patience, and the tenderness for their task in the years ahead.

May love be the constant companion of the home, and gentleness the handmaiden; and enfold them all in your peace, for Jesus' sake. *Stanley Pritchard*

See also 347

Our children: a parents' prayer **494**

Heavenly Father, we pray for our children growing up in this uncertain world, unsure of themselves or of their future, a world with grasping hands and debased values, a world without hope or security.

May we encourage our growing children to ask their questions, to think through their doubts, and to give tongue to their fears; may we help to nurture their faith and build up their trust in your loving purposes; and may we so live that the world they will inherit may be a better place than the world into which they were born. *Stanley Pritchard*

Marriage's dark days **495**

Loving Saviour, you taught us that all things are possible to our heavenly Father.

Strengthen our belief in your words, especially in the difficult days of our marriage when fears, mistrust and doubts arise.

Renew our spirits with fresh awakenings of love, joy, trust and forgiveness.

Increase our faith in the power of the Holy Spirit to make

all things new, that by his grace our marriage may be restored to its former joy, and together we may give you thanks and praise. *Mothers' Union Prayer Book*

Estrangement in a family **496**

Heavenly Father, whose will it is that your children should live in peace with you and in harmony with one another: look with compassion on the members of this family now suffering the pain of estrangement.

Give to all a desire for reconciliation;

remove every hindrance to true love and understanding;

and grant that they may find the joy of forgiving and being forgiven, even as they seek your own gracious pardon, through the merits of Jesus Christ our Redeemer.

Martin Parsons

497

Forgive us, Lord, when jealousy, greed, temper, or pride disturb the peace of our family.

Help us to find the right words and actions to soothe and heal the hurt.

Forgive us when we quarrel, and make us ready to forgive one another; and may harmony be restored to our married life, and peace rule in our home; for the sake of Jesus Christ our Lord. *Patricia Mitchell**

Marriage breakdown **498**

God our Father, whose patience is inexhaustible and love unconquerable, have mercy on those who now face the desolation of a broken marriage.

Take from their hearts all bitterness and recrimination.

Help them in their anguish of heart to seek your will and to make a right decision.

And so overrule past mistakes that all may yet be for their true good and for your glory; through Jesus Christ our Lord.

Martin Parsons

A wedding anniversary **499**

God of all grace, you gladden our hearts with the yearly celebration of our wedding day.

Thank you for the mercies of the past.

Help us to treasure the precious memories of your goodness and faithfulness over the years, and deepen our love for one another and our confidence in you.

We ask it in the name of him who brought joy to the wedding feast at Cana, Jesus Christ our Lord.

Martin Parsons

500

Heavenly Father, we pray for your servants *N.* and *N.* as they celebrate their wedding anniversary, that they may give thanks to you for all your goodness and loving-kindness to them, and for the love which binds them together as husband and wife.

May they remember with grateful hearts your gifts of home, family, and friends.

Help them to rejoice in their shared memories of joy and laughter, sadness and disappointment; and as they praise you for the past, may they trust you for the future; in the name of Jesus our Lord. *Mothers' Union Prayer Book**

For the blessing of a home: 336–7

LIFE'S LATER YEARS

Those facing retirement **501**

LORD, you give to every man his work by which to glorify you, and his rest from labour when the time of retirement comes: grant your blessing to this your servant who lays down the burden of *his* life's employment.

May *he* find other means of true satisfaction in life, and continue to serve you while strength shall last; and in the end may *he* find a welcome to the eternal home in which all serve you in peace and love; through Jesus Christ our Lord.

Martin Parsons

502

Heavenly Father, you have ordained that mankind should both work and rest: we pray for those whose working life is drawing to a close and who are now facing retirement.

Prepare them in mind and spirit for this change in their life's pattern, that their future days and years may be positive and creative, beneficial to the work of the Church, and rewarding to all who know them; for Jesus Christ's sake.

Michael Botting

503

Merciful Father, you have promised that your goodness and mercy will follow us all the days of our life.

We claim that promise for ourselves in these years of retirement.

Teach us how to adapt ourselves to a different pattern of life; show us how to occupy our greater leisure; open up for us fresh avenues of service; and may all our days be lived to your glory; through Jesus Christ our Lord. *Adapted*

Old age **504**

Eternal God, you have taught us that with you one day is as a thousand years, and a thousand years as one day: so teach us to number our days that we may apply our hearts unto wisdom.

Make us to know that our times are in your hand; and in your mercy grant that our closing days may be the best yet as we follow Christ in the path that leads to eternal day; for his name's sake. *Martin Parsons*

505

Lord, our days are fast speeding from us. Things we meant to do are still left undone, and we sometimes feel that our usefulness is finished as the fire of life dies within us.

And yet in your mercy it need not be so. We may still have rich years of fulfilment ahead of us if we allow our minds to be stretched and our hands to take up tasks within their strength.

Lord, we offer you all our tomorrows.

Open a new window for us and give us a fresh view of life.

Open a new door, and enable us to walk through it to opportunity and challenge.

Lord, may we count our years not in days but in the number of our friends. And make us thankful for all your goodness. *Stanley Pritchard*

A *thanksgiving at life's eventide* **506**

Lord, we give you thanks as we look back over the years and trace the pattern of our life.

So much that was puzzling is now made clear; and if we do not yet have the answer to all life's mystery, we know enough to accept that in all things you work for the good of those who love you.

Even the disappointments of life have been for the best.

Even the sadness of life has been tinged with comfort.

And the partings of life have been made easier by the sense of the nearness of those we have loved.

We bless the hand that guided.

We bless the heart that planned.

We rest in the love that sustains. *Stanley Pritchard*

IN TIME OF ILLNESS

At a sickbed **507**

LORD Jesus Christ, healer of man's body, mind and spirit, have compassion on this your servant now laid aside in illness.

Restore *him* in your mercy to health and strength.

Give *him* the assurance of your love and forgiveness.

May *he* know your presence near *him*, and your peace in *his* heart; for your name's sake. *Martin Parsons*

Before an operation **508**

Father, you have promised your children that when they pass through the deep waters you will be with them.

In that assurance we commend to you this your servant *N.* as *he* faces *his* operation.

Give *him* a quiet confidence in your love and power, and keep *him* in your peace.

Give to the medical team the wisdom and skill needful for their task; and in your great goodness bring all to a successful outcome, for the glory of your name; through Jesus Christ our Lord. *Martin Parsons*

In ill health **509**

Into your hands, O Lord, I commit myself
and all others who are ill.
Help us to realize that through your Passion
you understand our weakness and pain,
and that in your risen life
we also are lifted up to heavenly fellowship
by your Holy Spirit. *Henry Cooper*

510

O God my Father, help me to know that your healing life and power are within me.

Help me to do all that is in my power to help myself; and so help me to look forward to, and to expect, returning health and strength; through Jesus Christ our Lord.

Guild of Health

On recovery from illness **511**

O Lord our healer, whose will for your children is wholeness and healing: we praise you for the measure of renewed health you have granted to your servant *N.*

Continue your gracious work in *his* life; and bring *him* to a deeper knowledge of your love now, and to fullness of life in heaven hereafter; for Jesus Christ's sake. *Michael Botting*

Terminal illness **512**

Almighty God, whose Son Jesus Christ suffered and died for our salvation: in his name we commit into your hands this your servant *N.*

May *he* know your presence as he passes through the dark valley, that *he* may fear no evil.

Give *him* a firm trust in your forgiving love, and full assurance of eternal life through him who is the Resurrection and the Life, our Lord and Saviour Jesus Christ.

Martin Parsons

513

We thank you, our Father, that there is nothing in death or life that can separate us from your love, and that whether we live or die, we belong to you.

Give this confidence to your servant *N.*, whom we now lovingly remember and commend to your mercy and care; and grant *him* your peace to the journey's end: the peace that passes all understanding in Christ Jesus our Lord.

Frank Colquhoun

Bereavement **514**

O LORD, our heavenly Father, we pray for *those* whose life has been shattered by the death of *husband*, *wife*, or *child*.

Be with *them* in *their* loneliness and comfort *them* in *their* sorrow.

Grant *them* freedom from resentment, the courage and strength to seek your will in *their* new situation, and the faith to look beyond *their* present distress to Jesus, the one who conquered death and who lives for evermore.

Mothers' Union Prayer Book

515

O God our Father, whatever comes to us in life, help us to face it with courage and hope, knowing that you are always with us and that in perfect wisdom, perfect love, you are working for the best.

Help us at this time to think not of the darkness of death but of the splendour of the life everlasting in your presence.

Comfort and support us, strengthen and uphold us, until we meet again those we have loved and lost awhile; through Jesus Christ our Lord. *Edith Crowe*

516

Lord, I know that life can never be the same again. The one I loved has been taken from me, and I am conscious of an acute loneliness, an inner emptiness; and life seems to have lost its meaning.

Yet I know, Lord, that I am not alone, for you are with

me. And I know that my loved one is not dead or lost but is alive and safe in your keeping. And I know that death is not the end, and that life is still full of meaning, for your promises cannot fail and your love is unchanging.

Lord, I know these things. I ask you to make them real to me. Above all, I ask you to make yourself real to me at this time as my trusted Master and Friend; for while life may never be the same again, you are always the same: yesterday, and today, and for ever. *Frank Colquhoun*

The loss of a baby **517**

O God, whose ways are hidden from our sight, help us to believe that you make nothing in vain, and that you love all that you have made.

Comfort these your servants whose hearts are stricken and oppressed by their loss.

Make them to know that their child is safe in your keeping; and grant that they may so love and serve you in this life that in the end they may enter, with *him*, into the glory of your eternal kingdom; through the merits of your Son, our Saviour Jesus Christ. *Martin Parsons*

518

Father of all mercies and God of all comfort, whose ways are beyond our present understanding, we lay before you the grievous loss of our baby *N*.

Be close to us in our grief, and help us to resist the temptation to lose faith.

Make the cloud to lift and the darkness to clear; and through this mysterious tragedy fulfil your loving purpose for us and our family.

We ask it in the name of Jesus, who bowed to your will and trod the way of the cross. *Michael Botting*

519

Father, even though there is sorrow in our hearts today, we thank you for the life of this young child. You have a plan and purpose for every life, and ultimately nothing can spoil your plan or defeat your purpose.

When a child suffers through accident, through our lack of knowledge, or through handicap of body or mind, teach us that this is not your will for the little one. Such things happen; but even then your purposes are not finally frustrated, for this present life is only a part of the life you have prepared for us and for our children.

It is our faith that life extends beyond death, and that at last through your mercy the plan will be completed, the purpose fulfilled.

Father, strengthen this faith in us, and give us your peace in Jesus our Lord. *Stanley Pritchard*

For one reported lost or missing **520**

Most merciful Father, Redeemer of mankind, whose love for all your children is unchanging and unending: we commend to your love our dearest *N.*, in whatever state or place *he* may be.

Fulfil in *him*, O Lord, your own gracious work and perfect will, that *he* may find your peace; and grant that we may be reunited with *him* in this present life, if such be your will, or at last in the joy of your presence hereafter; through the merits of our Saviour Jesus Christ.

Frank Colquhoun

Life's dark valleys **521**

Loving Father, we know that life's journey sometimes leads through dark valleys, and that many are travelling that path just now, even as we are.

Help us to remember that however dark the valley, the

darkness does not hide us from you. May it not hide you from us, but may we know that you are always near us, sharing our burden and entering into our grief.

Help us also to remember that the valley will not go on for ever: that with you by our side we shall at length emerge from it, and the darkness will lift, and we shall yet praise you, our Saviour and our God. *Frank Colquhoun*

VARIOUS

Going to university or college **522**

HEAVENLY Father, we pray for those who are about to enter upon a new life as students at university or college.

Teach them to use their greater freedom as good stewards of time and opportunity.

Bless them in their studies, sanctify their leisure, and enrich them with true friendships.

May your love in Christ be the inspiration of all they do, so that their life of service in after years may be for your honour and glory. *Martin Parsons*

Starting work **523**

Lord God, your strength is made perfect in our weakness.

May this be the confidence of those who are now beginning work or starting a new job.

Give them grace to serve you in serving others, that work and worship may be one great offering to your glory; in the name of him who finished the work you gave him to do, Jesus Christ our Lord. *Martin Parsons*

Moving away from the parish **524**

Holy Spirit of God, inspirer of all that is good and true in life, we ask you to be with our friends . . . who are leaving this neighbourhood and moving to a new home.

May they soon become part of their community and make new friends.

We give thanks for all that they have contributed here, and pray that they may continue to know your presence and peace. *Mothers' Union Prayer Book*

525

O God, you lead your people as a shepherd leads his flock: we thank you for your mercies to us while we have lived in this area, for friendships made, for joys and sorrows shared.

Be with us as we move to our new home, and direct us into fresh avenues of service.

Teach us to venture trustfully into the future while we retain our gratitude for the past. Above all, make us to live each present moment in ways pleasing to you; for the sake of Jesus Christ our Lord. *Martin Parsons*

Those lacking spiritual assurance **526**

Loving Shepherd, you have promised that no one shall ever pluck your sheep out of your hand.

Speak this word of assurance to those who are doubtful of their salvation.

Show them the truth of the gospel, that they may rest their faith in the sufficiency of your atoning death and rejoice in the victory of your resurrection.

So may they look away from their fears and failings to you, the author and finisher of their faith, the same yesterday, and today, and for ever. *Martin Parsons*

Making a decision **527**

Lord, two choices are before me, and I'm afraid to choose
in case I make the wrong decision.
I have examined the facts and consulted the experts;
I have talked over the issues with my friends;
but I am no nearer a decision.
If I knew what next year held for me
there would be no problem in making the right choice;
but I do not know, and there is no one to guide me.
So help me, Lord, with my decisions.
I know that you will not, in your wisdom,
show me all the way ahead;
but you will give me lantern light for the next step.
Illumine the footprints my feet can follow,
and make me content to take one step at a time.

Stanley Pritchard

XI
DEVOTIONAL PRAYERS

MORNING AND EVENING

In the morning **528**

God and Father of us all, from whom alone we have the desire and the power to live aright: grant that the clean page of this new day may remain unspotted to the end; and that whatever is recorded upon it by our lives may prove worthy to be treasured in our memories; so that at the day's closing we may present it unashamed to you; through Jesus Christ our Lord. *Douglas Horsefield*

529

Into your strong hands, our Father,
we commend this day
our souls and bodies,
our homes and families,
our friends and neighbours,
and all who specially need your help.
Grant to each of us your all-sufficient grace,
and keep us in peace and safety;
through Jesus Christ our Lord.

530

May we accept this day at your hand, O God,
as a gift to be treasured,
a life to be enjoyed,
a trust to be kept,
and a hope to be fulfilled;
and all for your glory. *Stanley Pritchard*

531

O God, help me this day
to use the brains you have given me
without pride,
the hands you have given me
without sloth,
and the tongue you have given me
without malice;
for Jesus Christ's sake. *Stanley Pritchard*

532

This day help us to praise you, O God,
for your goodness and loving-kindness,
and all the blessings of this life.
This day help us to trust you, O God,
in every circumstance of life,
with hearts that are steadfast and strong.
This day help us to serve you, O God,
with love and faithfulness,
with all our powers of body, mind and spirit.
This day help us to glorify you, O God,
in all our thoughts and words and actions,
from the beginning to the end;
through Jesus Christ our Lord. *Adapted*

533

Fill us, O Lord, with your Holy Spirit, that we may go forth this day with eagerness and joy, to love and serve you in holiness, and to do your perfect will; for Christ our Saviour's sake. *Harold E. Evans*

534

Help us, O God, to live this day
  quietly, hopefully;
to lean on your strength
  trustfully, restfully;
to wait for the unfolding of your will
  patiently, serenely;
to meet other people
  peacefully, joyfully;
to face every task
  confidently, courageously;
in the name of Christ our Lord.

*Cringleford Mothers' Union**

At evening **535**

Blessed are you, O Lord, the God of our fathers, creator of the changes of day and night, giving rest to the weary, renewing the strength of those who are spent, bestowing upon us occasions of song in the evening.

As you have protected us in the day that is past, so be with us in the coming night. Keep us from every sin, every evil, and every fear; for you are our light and salvation, and the strength of our life.

To you be glory for endless ages.

Episcopal Church, U.S.A.

536

At this evening hour, O Lord our God, we remember with thankful hearts your care and protection and all the blessings we have received in the day that is past.

In your mercy forgive us any wrong we have done, any evil thoughts we have harboured, any unkind words we have spoken.

Have in your safe keeping this night those we love; comfort and relieve the sick, the suffering, and the sorrowful; and give us all the benediction of your peace; through Jesus Christ our Lord. *Adapted*

537

Our Father, we come to you at the ending of the day with thankful hearts, to commit ourselves and those we love to your care and protection for the coming night.

Lift from our minds every burden, every anxiety, every fear; and in your great mercy give us sleep and rest to fit us for the duties of another day; through our Lord and Saviour Jesus Christ. *Adapted*

DAILY LIFE

Life's pilgrimage **538**

TEACH us, O God, to view our life here on earth
as a pilgrim's path to heaven,
and give us grace to tread it courageously
in the company of your faithful people.
Help us to set our affections on the things above,
not on the passing vanities of this world;
and grant that as we journey on in the way of holiness
we may bear a good witness to our Lord,
and serve all who need our help along the way,
for the glory of your name.

Frank Colquhoun

Our talents **539**

We thank you, our Father, for the varied talents you have given to your children: to some the gift of music or painting, to others of writing or athletic skills.

Above all we thank you for the greater gifts of understanding, sympathy and friendship, which can bring help and happiness to others.

Show each of us what are your special gifts to us, and enable us to use them for your glory; through Christ our Lord.

The stewardship of time **540**

Teach us, O Lord, to use your gifts
with wisdom and generosity.
Teach us also to use our time
carefully and effectively,
not as a miser, nor as a spendthrift,
but as those who know that time is a gift
to be accounted for in the end of the day.

Stanley Pritchard

Profit and loss **541**

Lord Christ, you have taught us that it profits us nothing if we gain the whole world and lose our own souls.

Make us willing so to lose ourselves for your sake, that we may find ourselves anew in the life of grace; and so to forget ourselves that we may be remembered in your eternal kingdom; for your name's sake. *Adapted*

Our life . . . **542**

Father of all mercies,
we bless you for our creation.
The life we possess is your gift:
we hold it in trust from you.
Teach us to value it and to use it to the full.
For we have but one life to live on earth,
one life in which to glorify you,
to serve your Church,
to advance your kingdom,
to help other people.
Lord, show us what to do with our life,
and let us not live to be useless. *Frank Colquhoun*

. . . and our death **543**

Lord Jesus Christ, we thank you
that in sharing our life here on earth
you also entered into the experience of death.
As we trust you with our life,
may we likewise trust you with our death.
When our time comes to tread the dark valley,
grant that we may fear no evil
but may know that you are with us,
and will at last receive us to yourself,
so that where you are we may be also,
in our Father's house for evermore. *Frank Colquhoun*

Speech . . . **544**

"Set a guard, O Lord, on my mouth,
and keep the door of my lips."
Father, we should make our own
this prayer of the psalmist.
Save us from foolish or hurtful talk,
from uttering lies or making false promises.
Give us the courage to say what we mean,
and the honesty to mean what we say.
And may our speech always be seasoned with grace,
that it may bring a blessing to those who hear it;
through Jesus Christ our Lord. *Frank Colquhoun*
Psalm 141.3; Ephesians 4.29; Colossians 3.9; 4.6

. . . and silence **545**

Lord, you have taught us in your word
that there is a time to speak
and a time to keep silence.
As we thank you for the power of speech,
we pray also for the grace of silence.
Make us as ready to listen as we are to talk:

ready to listen to your voice
in the quietness of our hearts,
and ready to listen to other people
who need a sympathetic ear.
Show us when to open our mouths
and when to hold our peace,
that we may glorify you
both in speech and in silence;
through Jesus Christ our Lord.

Frank Colquhoun

Self **546**

Lord, we confess that we ourselves
are our own worst enemies.
We know there is too much of self in our lives:
self-righteousness and self-centredness,
self-indulgence and self-deception.
Save us, O Lord, from ourselves, and lead us
in the way of self-denial,
self-discipline and self-sacrifice.
And as we learn to dethrone self,
help us to enthrone Christ
and crown him Lord of all,
our glorious King for ever. *Frank Colquhoun*

Influence **547**

Help us, O Lord, to remember that you have given us the power of influencing others for good or for evil: of tempting them to do wrong or of encouraging them in all that is right and good.

May we never lead others astray by what we say or do, but may our lives always be a wholesome influence for goodness and righteousness, both in our homes and in the places where we live and work; for Jesus Christ's sake. *Adapted*

Life and work **548**

Inspire and direct us, O God, to seek and to do your will in all the common affairs of life:

in our homes, that purity and love may be guarded;

in our relations with others, that peace and harmony may prevail;

in our work, that truth and justice may be honoured;

and in our hearts, that Christ alone may reign there; for the glory of your name.

549

O God, we thank you for the gift of life
and for the faculties which enable us to enjoy it.
You have given us our eyes to see the beauty of your world,
our ears to hear speech and the sound of music,
our lips with which to speak in friendship to others,
and our hands with which to minister to their needs.
Help us, through the grace of your Holy Spirit,
to use all that we have in your service
and for your greater glory;
through Jesus Christ our Lord. *Adapted*

550

O God, give us work
till our life shall end,
and give us life till our work is done;
for Jesus Christ's sake.

God's workmanship **551**

All your works praise you, O Lord,
and we would add our voices to their praise.
For we are your workmanship,

created in your image,
created for your glory,
created to serve your kingdom.
Fulfil in us and through us, Lord God,
the purposes of your love,
and help us in our daily lives
to reflect more of your likeness;
through Jesus Christ our Lord. *Frank Colquhoun*

Psalm 145.10; Ephesians 2.10

PRAYERS OF DEDICATION

The life of service **552**

GOD of all grace, we thank you for the many skills of body and mind that you have given us.

We gratefully offer them in the service of your purpose for all mankind, for the welfare and prosperity of our fellow men, and for the honour and glory of your name.

Basil Naylor

553

Heavenly Father, we thank you for calling us
to be your servants.
Help us gladly to respond to your call
and to obey your will.
Make us ready for every demand
you make upon our lives,
that we may serve you faithfully
and show forth your love to the world;
through Jesus Christ our Lord.

554

Help us, O Lord, by your grace, to fulfil the purpose for which in your wisdom you created us and in your love you redeemed us; that all our days here upon earth may be of service to others and accomplish something of worth for your kingdom and your glory; through our Lord and Saviour Jesus Christ. *Frank Colquhoun*

555

God our Father, so possess our hearts,
 guide our minds
 and strengthen our wills,
that we may give ourselves to you
 in thankfulness and love,
and be used in the service of your kingdom;
 for Jesus Christ's sake.

The dedicated heart **556**

Grant us, O Lord our God,
 to you – a heart of flame;
 to our fellow men – a heart of love;
 to ourselves – a heart of steel.
We ask it in Christ's name.

Adapted from St. Augustine

Love's response **557**

Thank you, O God, for your love,
 and for all that you have done for me.
Help me to do more for you,
 and to live only and always for your glory;
for Jesus Christ's sake. *Frank Colquhoun*

VARIOUS GRACES

Love for God **558**

O GOD, we love you
because you first loved us.
Yet our love for you is so feeble,
while your love for us is so strong.
Teach us more of your love
that we may love you better;
and help us to show our love for you
by our love for others,
even as you love both them and us,
in Jesus Christ our Lord.

Frank Colquhoun

Love for others **559**

Grant us, O God our Father,
the love that is always ready to forgive;
the love that is always ready to help;
the love that delights to give rather than to get.
And so grant that, living in love,
we may live like Jesus.

560

O God of love, we ask you to give us love:
love in our thinking,
love in our speaking,
love in our doing,
and love in the hidden places of our souls.

Love of our neighbours and our friends,
love for those with whom we find it hard to bear,
and love for those who find it hard to bear with us.
  Love in joy and love in sorrow,
  love in life and love in death;
that so at length we may be worthy
to dwell with you, Eternal Love,
through him who reveals your love,
  Jesus Christ our Lord. *After William Temple*

561

Most merciful Father,
  keep the door of our hearts,
  that only love may enter them;
and keep the door of our lips,
  that only love may speak through them;
for Christ our Saviour's sake.

Faith **562**

Father, as we remember the victorious faith of your servants of old, we acknowledge that we are not people of faith.

Sometimes your promises seem so unlikely as to be laughable. They are almost more than we can believe.

Father, forgive us. Increase our faith, and save us from concentrating on our doubts.

Open our eyes to see what you can do with us when we put ourselves at your disposal.

Help us to hold firm to your promises, to laugh at impossibilities, and to believe that all things are possible, through Jesus Christ our Lord.

563

O Lord, strengthen the faith of us who believe,
and sow the seed of faith in the hearts of those who lack it.
Give us grace to show our faith by our works;
teach us to walk by faith, in reliance on your promises;
and enable us to fight the good fight of faith,
that by faith we may overcome the world,
through him who loved us, and whose love is without end,
our Lord and Saviour Jesus Christ.

After Christina Rossetti

An act of faith **564**

We believe in God the Father,
Creator of all that is,
whose mystery is beyond our understanding,
whose love is always around us.
We believe in God the Son,
Jesus the incarnate Word,
who suffered and died for us,
our risen and living Lord.
We believe in God the Holy Spirit,
Spirit of truth and love,
God's power in the Church and the world,
within our hearts to strengthen and sanctify.
Glory be to the Father, the Son, and the Holy Spirit,
now and for ever.

Sympathy **565**

Grant us grace, our Father, not to pass by suffering or joy without eyes to see them.

Give us understanding and sympathy, and guard us from selfishness.

Help us to enter into the joys and sorrows of others; and

use us to gladden and strengthen those who are weak and suffering; for the sake of Christ our Lord.

After Dick Sheppard

Sincerity **566**

Save us, O Lord, from being self-righteous and self-satisfied: from pretending to be other than we really are.

Help us to recognize our faults and admit our mistakes.

Give us a burning shame for those evil things we condemn in others and are so quick to excuse in ourselves; and make us honest men and women, that we may serve you in sincerity and truth; for Jesus Christ's sake. *Adapted*

Thankfulness **567**

Forgive me, Lord, for a mind
that turns so readily to weigh my troubles,
so seldom to count my blessings.
Teach me the practice of recollection,
the habit of thankfulness,
the art of praise.
And may I deal as generously with others
as you deal with me;
for Jesus Christ's sake. *Timothy Dudley-Smith*

Christian joy **568**

God of hope, fill us with all joy as well as with all peace in believing; that we may serve you with gladness, delight to do your will, and always make melody to you in our hearts; through Jesus Christ our Lord. *Frank Colquhoun*

Freedom from fear **569**

Lord, you have taught us to trust and not be afraid:
deliver us from fear of the unknown future,
fear of failure and poverty,

fear of sickness and pain,
fear of bereavement and loneliness,
fear of old age and fear of death.
Help us, our Father, to love and fear you alone,
that with strong faith and cheerful courage
we may commit ourselves and all the days to come
into your safe keeping,
in the name of Christ our Lord.

Morning, Noon and Night★

The presence of Christ **570**

Come to us, Lord Christ, in your understanding love
when all around us seems dark and uncertain,
when our faith is low and we cannot feel you near,
and we find it hard to pray.
Come to us then, dear Lord,
as you came to your disciples,
in the darkest hour of the night,
and let the light of your presence dispel our fears,
renew our trust, and bring peace to our hearts,
for your tender mercies' sake. *Frank Colquhoun*

The peace of Christ **571**

Lord Christ, eternal peace and bond of all peace,
who gave and entrusted to your disciples
that peace which you wish us to maintain on earth:
pour into our hearts the gift of the Holy Spirit,
that as he dwells in us
disputes may die,
discord vanish,
anger take flight,
and love seize hold of all that is ours,
now and for ever. *Adapted from Mozarabic Liturgy*

A tranquil mind **572**

Heavenly Father, in this age of noise and speed and restless activity, grant us tranquillity: the inner tranquillity of spirit which is theirs who trust in your sovereign love and wisdom; that as the life of the world surges around us, we may yet be still and know that you are God; through Jesus Christ our Lord. *Frank Colquhoun*

Intelligence **573**

Help us, Lord God, to make the best use of the intelligence you have given us, that we may act as rational beings in time of crisis or emergency.

Give us also sanctified common sense in our everyday affairs, that we may not cause trouble to ourselves or others by our lack of understanding; and enable us to know the right way of doing things and the right words to say, as servants of your Son, our Lord and Saviour Jesus Christ.

A sense of humour **574**

Give us a sense of humour, Lord,
and also things to laugh about.
Give us the grace to take a joke against ourselves
and to see the funny side of life.
Save us from annoyance, bad temper,
or resentfulness against our friends.
Help us to laugh even in the face of trouble;
and fill our minds with the love of Jesus,
for his name's sake. *A. G. Bullivant*

575

Dear Lord, thank you for one of the greatest of all your many gifts to us – a sense of humour. Teach us to value it and to use it for the building up of your kingdom of joy and hope on earth; for Jesus' sake. *Alan Warren*

The fruit of the Spirit **576**

Grant to us, Lord, lives marked by faithfulness,
by gentleness and self-control;
by patience, kindness and goodness
towards all we meet;
and by love, joy, peace
within our hearts.
So may the Spirit of Christ bear fruit in us;
for his name's sake. *Timothy Dudley-Smith*

The new life in Christ **577**

Heavenly Father, by uniting us with Christ
you have made us new creatures:
the old life is over,
the new life has begun.
Help us to enter more deeply into this experience,
that through Christ we may die to sin,
live to truth and righteousness,
and be daily renewed by your Holy Spirit,
to the honour of your name.

Imitators of Christ **578**

Lord Christ, help us to follow more closely in your footsteps, that we may reflect in our own lives the love and obedience which you have shown us in yours; for your name's sake.

OUR FATHER

Our Father's name **579**

GIVE to your children, Lord, a true concern for the honour of your name, and a proper reverence for all holy things.

May we who bear that name, and seek to serve it, be kept from all betrayal or denial; and may the love of your name move us in turn to love; through Jesus Christ our Lord.

Timothy Dudley-Smith

His kingdom **580**

O God, whose kingdom is not of this world and yet is found among us where Christ is named as Lord, teach us to set your kingdom above all self-interest and the personal ambitions which captivate our hearts.

Help us to seek and serve it in quiet ways, that we may stand firm as your loyal and faithful subjects when trouble comes; through Jesus Christ our Lord.

Timothy Dudley-Smith

His will **581**

O Father, whose love has given free will to every human soul, teach us in love to choose your will as ours; through Jesus Christ our Lord. *Timothy Dudley-Smith*

Daily bread **582**

Father of all mercies, we thank you for your loving concern for us your children and for your daily provision for our bodily needs.

Keep us always mindful of our dependence on your goodness and bounty, and teach us in turn to care for the wants of others, in the name of Jesus our Lord.

Frank Colquhoun

Forgiveness **583**

God of all grace, we pray that as we daily seek and receive your full and free forgiveness of our sins, so we may as fully and freely forgive those who do us wrong; and may we offer our forgiveness, even as you grant us yours, for the sake of our Saviour Jesus Christ. *Frank Colquhoun*

Temptation **584**

Heavenly Father, we confess how weak we are in ourselves as we face temptation, and how strong are the forces of evil in the world around us.

Daily and hourly gird us with your strength, that we may be saved from sinning and be victorious over every foe; for yours, O Lord, is the power, as yours also is the kingdom and the glory, for ever and ever. *Frank Colquhoun*

ACKNOWLEDGMENTS

THE Editor wishes to express his thanks to the following for permission to reproduce or adapt prayers of which they are the authors or publishers.

The Episcopal Church of the United States of America for prayers from the revised edition (1977) of the Book of Common Prayer.

The Church Missionary Society for prayers adapted from *Morning, Noon and Night* (1976), edited by John Carden, and for other prayers.

The United Society for the Propagation of the Gospel and Canon John Kingsnorth for prayers written by him in the society's magazine *Network* and *Prayers for Mission*.

The Church Pastoral Aid Society for prayers from the first edition of *Prayers for Today's Church* (1972), edited by Dick Williams.

The Mothers' Union for prayers from the *Mothers' Union Prayer Book* and the *Mothers' Union Service Book*.

Hodder and Stoughton for prayers, slightly adapted, from *A House of Private Prayer* (1958) by Leslie D. Weatherhead.

The Guild of Health and the Guild of St Raphael for prayers dealing with the ministry of healing.

Acknowledgment for the use of prayers is also made to the following persons: Bishop George Appleton, Bishop Hugh Blackburne, Prebendary Henry Cooper, the Rev. Dr Andrew Doig, Cardinal Basil Hume, the Rev. Michael Perry, Archbishop Robert Runcie, the Rev.

John R. W. Stott, Canon F. W. Street, the Rev. Norman Wallwork, the Rev. Andrew Warner; and to the following societies and organizations: Advisory Council for the Church's Ministry, Anglican Pacifist Fellowship, Bible Reading Fellowship, British and Foreign Bible Society, British Council of Churches, Christian Aid, Feed the Minds, Missions to Seamen, Order of Christian Unity.

INDEX OF SOURCES

References are to the numbers prefixed to the prayers

INDEX OF SUBJECTS